THE BASEBALL BOOK

A complete A-to-Z informal encyclopedia of baseball, with the greatest moments, all-time stars, team histories, and winning techniques—plus the colorful language and timeless stories of America's favorite sport. Lavishly illustrated with photographs.

THE
Baseball
BOOK

edited by Zander Hollander

ILLUSTRATED WITH PHOTOGRAPHS

A Zander Hollander Sports Book

Random House New York

Some of the material included here originally
appeared in *The Encyclopedia of Sports Talk,*
edited by Zander Hollander,
Copyright © 1976 by Associated Features Inc.

Library of Congress Cataloging in Publication Data:
Main entry under title:
The Baseball book.
"A Zander Hollander sports book."
Summary: An encyclopedia of baseball's great moments,
stars, teams, techniques, language, and anecdotes.
1. Baseball—United States—Dictionaries, Juvenile.
[1. Baseball—Dictionaries] I. Hollander, Zander.
GV867.5.B37   796.357′03   81-14384
ISBN: 0-394-84296-0 (pbk.); 0-394-94296-5 (lib. bdg.)
AACR2

Photograph credits appear on page 160.

Book design by Kathleen Westray
Manufactured in the United States of America
1 2 3 4 5 6 7 8 9 0

Acknowledgments

Baseball is a team game with nine to a side. The editor acknowledges with appreciation the winning nine who contributed to *The Baseball Book:* Howard Blatt, Hal Bock, Eric Compton, Phyllis Hollander, Frank Kelly, Dennis Lyons, Phil Pepe, Bill Roeder, and Debbie Zwecher.

Play Ball!

Let's get *aboard* for a trip *around the horn* to the *World Series*. Along the way there will be stops at the *hot corner*, the *Hall of Fame*, the *Grapefruit League*, the *victory party*, and *Death Valley*, among other places.

You'll meet *Charlie Hustle*, the *Junk Man*, the *Gashouse Gang*, the *Phantom Infield*, and *Casey at the Bat*.

These are only a few of the 400 entries—from Hank Aaron to Carl Yastrzemski—that you'll find on your journey through *The Baseball Book*. The goal of the editors was to touch all the bases: to tell the stories of the superstars, the great moments, and the teams; to define the colorful language of the game; and to provide the records on which baseball legends are built.

Whether you play it or watch it at the ballpark or on television; whether you're new to the sport and want to learn about it or are a seasoned fan, this book is designed to answer your questions while giving you a laugh or two along the way.

Since the entries are alphabetical, you can easily look things up. If you're following a particular player or team, check the index at the back because many names appear in more than one entry. And, of course, you can simply browse through the pages and discover why baseball is our national pastime.

—Zander Hollander

● *This was the swing that made history on April 8, 1974, in Atlanta.*

AARON, HANK. With a seeming sense of the dramatic, Hank Aaron of the Atlanta Braves had finished the 1973 season with 713 career home runs, one short of one of baseball's most cherished records, the 714 hit by the immortal Babe Ruth.

All winter the anticipation grew, and finally the 1974 season began—with Atlanta in Cincinnati on April 4. In his very first time at bat, against Jack Billingham, Aaron hit a sinking fastball over the left-center-field fence to tie the Babe.

Four days later in Atlanta, at exactly 9:07 P.M., on an overcast, windy, cool evening, before 52,780 screamers who came to see history, Henry Louis Aaron slugged a fast-ball delivered by Los Angeles Dodger left-hander Al Downing. The ball soared over the left-center-field fence and Hank had his record-smashing 715th.

Two years later Aaron ended his fabulous 23-year career, finishing with a record total of 755 home runs. Less well known is the fact that Aaron also finished as the all-time leader in runs batted in with 2,297, number 2 in runs scored with 2,174, and number 2 in hits with 3,771.

Aaron was born on February 5, 1934, in Mobile, Alabama, and came to the majors in 1954 as an outfielder with the Milwaukee Braves. He was slender and did not look like a power hitter. But he had developed the ability to snap his wrists as he swung, and those fast wrists would get him his record number of home runs.

Aaron won two batting championships, led the league in RBI's three times, and was the home-run king four times. And his good hitting was continuous. Eight times he hit 40 or more homers, and 10 times he drove in over 100 runs in a single season. He was the greatest power hitter of his time and finished his career with a .305 batting average.

● *When Hank Aaron hit his 715th home run, it was a blow heard 'round the baseball world.*

ABOARD. On base. When a team has a man on base, it is said to have a man aboard. So a team may have nobody aboard (bases empty) or it may have one, two, or three runners aboard.

AGENT. Someone who negotiates baseball or other contracts for players for a fee. In the case of bonus players, the agent (often a lawyer) is the bargainer between the ballclub and the player, and his fee is a percentage (usually from 10 to 20 percent) of the bonus.

Among established stars the agent may negotiate a contract or he may set up television commercials for the player. The agent is paid a percentage of the player's fee.

So when you see George Brett on television praising a soft drink, or Pete Rose telling you why he uses a certain aftershave lotion, be assured that the athlete is being well paid for his advice and that an agent is getting his share of the fee.

● *Connie Mack (left), American League, and John McGraw, National League, were the opposing managers in the first All-Star Game in 1933.*

ALL-STAR GAME. In 1933 Arch Ward, sports editor of the Chicago *Tribune*, seeking to add a baseball flavor to Chicago's hundredth birthday celebration, had the idea that fans would like to see a game between the best players of the National League and the best from the American League. So on July 6, 1933, the first All-Star Game was played at Chicago's Comiskey Park. The American League won the game on a two-run home run by Babe Ruth. Lefty Gomez of the New York Yankees was the winning pitcher.

The All-Star Game became an annual attraction and has been played every year since it began, except for 1945, when the game was called off because of World War II. In 1959 the players of both leagues voted to play two All-Star Games and did so until 1963, when, realizing they were making the

● *The Dodgers' Don Drysdale, throwing in the 1968 classic, holds the record for most innings pitched, 19, and most strikeouts, 19, in All-Star Game history.*

12 ●

game less appealing, they went back to one game a year.

Part of the earnings from the All-Star Game goes to the players' pension fund, which is one reason players have no objection to playing on what would otherwise be a day of rest. Another reason is the honor that goes along with selection. Stan Musial, Willie Mays, and Hank Aaron share the record of having played in the most All-Star Games —24.

The American League dominated the All-Star Game in the beginning, winning the first 3 and 12 of the first 16. However, the National League has won 29 of the next 36 (there was one tie) through 1981.

The most memorable All-Star Game occurred in 1934 at New York's Polo Grounds. Pitching in his home park, Carl Hubbell, a New York Giant left-hander, struck out one after the other the mighty Babe Ruth, Lou Gehrig, Jimmie Foxx, Al Simmons, and Joe Cronin.

AMERICAN LEAGUE. This is the younger of baseball's two major leagues; the other is the National League. The American League was first thought of in 1892,

although it was not formed until nine years later.

In 1892 Charles Albert Comiskey, player-manager for the Cincinnati Red Stockings, and Byron Bancroft (Ban) Johnson, baseball columnist for the Cincinnati *Gazette,* began to grow unhappy with the old-fashioned and large 12-team National League and started thinking of forming a league of their own.

Comiskey talked up the idea of bringing back the old Western Association, an earlier league, with a new name, to compete with the National League. Interest was great among owners, and Comiskey recommended Johnson as president of the new league.

Even with the imaginative and energetic Johnson at the head, the new league moved slowly until 1899, when the National League dropped four teams. Johnson added the four teams to his league and changed the name from the Western Association to the American League, and on April 24, 1901, the American League began operations with a gala opening game in which Cleveland played Chicago in Chicago.

Charter members of the American League in 1901 were Chicago (first American League champion), Boston, Detroit, Philadelphia, Baltimore, Washington, Cleveland, and Milwaukee.

The next year Milwaukee was replaced by St. Louis, and in 1903 John McGraw, one of the owners of the Baltimore club, sold his share of the team and went back to the National League to head the New York Giants. Johnson's reply was defiance. He moved the Baltimore franchise to New York in direct competition with the Giants, despite politicians' threats to run city streets through his ballpark.

In 1903 the American League included eight teams, which stayed in the same cities until the 1954 season, when the St. Louis Browns asked for and received permission to move to Baltimore. The following year the Philadelphia Athletics moved to Kansas City.

• *Ron Guidry of the Yankees was one of the American League's premier pitchers in the late 1970s.*

heim (site of Disneyland) and opened the 1966 season in their new home. To create broader appeal the Angels changed their name from the Los Angeles Angels to the California Angels.

In 1968 the Kansas City club moved to Oakland, and a year later the American League expanded to 12 teams with a new franchise in Kansas City and another in Seattle. The league was split into two divisions, East and West, and the winning teams of both divisions played each other for the league championship. The winner of those playoffs represented the league in the World Series.

The Seattle franchise was moved to Milwaukee in 1970, and the Washington, D.C., club moved to Texas two years later. Eventually the Eastern Division listed New York, Baltimore, Boston, Cleveland, Detroit, and Milwaukee. Minnesota, California, Chicago, Kansas City, Oakland, and Texas were in the Western Division. Toronto (Eastern Division) and a new Seattle team (Western Division) joined the league in 1977.

Under the guidance of Ban Johnson the American League thrived once it got off the ground, but Johnson's failure to get along with baseball commissioner Kenesaw Mountain Landis caused Johnson to resign in 1927. He was succeeded by Ernest S. Barnard, who reigned until his death in 1931 (the same year Ban Johnson died). On Barnard's death, Will Harridge was promoted from American League secretary to league president. Harridge resigned after the 1958 season, and in 1959 Joe Cronin became the American League president. In 1973 Cronin became chairman of the board of the American League and was succeeded as president by Leland (Lee) MacPhail.

In 1961 the American League voted to expand to 10 teams. To achieve this, the Washington Senators moved to the twin cities of Minneapolis–St. Paul and were called the Minnesota Twins, and new franchises were awarded to Los Angeles and Washington. Players for the two new teams were taken from a pool contributed by the eight established teams. Each team submitted a list of available players, from which the Los Angeles Angels and the Washington Senators could purchase players to stock their teams. The season schedule was increased from 154 games to 162.

In 1965 the Angels moved out of Los Angeles in a dispute with that city's National League team, the Dodgers. The Angels had been tenants of Dodger Stadium and considered the rental much too high. They constructed a new stadium in nearby Ana-

APPEAL. A claim by a member of the defensive team of a violation of the rules by the offensive team when such a violation is not automatically penalized. Example: if a batter bats out of turn or a runner fails to touch a base, the umpire cannot call the batter or runner out unless the defensive team appeals to the umpire.

AROUND THE HORN. A double play completed from the third baseman to the second baseman to the first baseman. The expression originated from the fact that it is the longest way to make a double play, just as the route around Cape Horn at the tip of South America, was the longest one from the Atlantic Ocean to the Pacific Ocean (and the only route until the Panama Canal was built).

ASPIRIN TABLET. A slang expression hitters use to explain what a ball thrown by Nolan Ryan (at more than 100 miles per hour) looks like when it comes up to the plate. It's not difficult to swallow, but it sure is tough to hit.

ASSIST. Official credit given in the scoring of a game to a player who throws or deflects a batted or thrown ball so that a putout results or would have resulted except for an error on the play. In the case of a deflection, the player must slow the ball down or change its direction to rate an assist.

Assists by infielders are common; they are relatively uncommon by outfielders, since it means throwing a runner out while he is trying to take an extra base or throwing a man out to complete a double play after an outfield catch.

The record for most outfield assists in one season is 44, set in 1930 by Chuck Klein of the Philadelphia Phillies. The record for most outfield assists in one game is four and is held by many players. The record for most outfield assists in one inning is two and is also held by many players.

AT-BAT. An official turn at hitting charged to a player except when he receives a base on balls, is hit by a pitched ball, makes a sacrifice hit, or is interfered with by the catcher.

ATLANTA BRAVES. Winding up his third World Series victory with his twenty-fourth shutout inning in a row, Lew Burdette had given the Milwaukee fans something special to celebrate in 1957. Five years after leaving Boston and 43 years after the last world championship in the franchise's history, the Braves had defeated the Yankees in a seven-game World Series.

The following year a Braves team led by pitchers Burdette and Warren Spahn and batters Hank Aaron and Eddie Mathews blew a 3–1 Series lead to the Yankees to lose in seven games. And in 1959 the Braves lost a three-game pennant playoff to the Dodgers.

By 1966 the love affair between the city of Milwaukee and the Braves was over, and the club moved to Atlanta. Apart from a division-winning season in 1969, the team's fans have had little to cheer about—other than the hitting exploits of home-run king Aaron.

The Miracle Braves of 1914, who were in last place halfway through the season and wound up winning the pennant by 10½ games, rode the hitting of Joe Connolly, the fielding of Rabbit Maranville, and the pitching of Dick Rudolph and Bill James to a Series sweep of the Philadelphia Athletics.

● *The Braves' Lew Burdette is throwing a no-hitter against the Phillies in 1960.*

In the four games Philadelphia scored a total of six runs.

In 1948, sustained by the pitching of Spahn and Johnny Sain, the Braves won a pennant, but lost the World Series in six games to Cleveland.

The only pitcher who has brought back memories of Spahn, Burdette, and Sain during the Braves' more recent history is Phil Niekro, who has knuckleballed his way to more than 230 career victories.

AUTOMATIC STRIKE. This is a pitch delivered with a count of three balls and no strikes. It is usually a called strike, since the pitcher simply tries to get it over and the batter is usually under orders not to swing on the chance that either it will be a ball or the pitcher is unlikely to throw two more strikes in a row. It is considered automatic because the pitcher is deliberately aiming for the strike zone without using his most effective pitch. The pitcher does this because he knows that the batter will probably not swing. Also called a cripple.

BACKSTOP. The catcher. Also, a screened structure behind home plate to stop foul balls from going into the stands.

BAIL OUT. When a pitch comes too close for comfort and the batter pulls away quickly to escape being hit, it is called bailing out. Sometimes it is used to put down a batter. If a batter bails out unnecessarily too often, it shows he is afraid of being hit, and pitchers will work on that weakness to keep him away from the plate.

BALK. This is a time-honored accusation that comes ringing from the stands whenever the pitcher makes a false move or what looks like one. But the umpire hardly ever calls it a balk. How come?

The answer usually lies in the pitcher's relationship to the pitching plate or rubber. As long as he is not standing on the rubber, the pitcher can make almost any move he pleases, including the business of wheeling toward a base and pretending to throw or even charging toward the runner—and these are what many fans think are balks. The pitcher almost always remembers to step off the rubber before trying such tactics.

A balk can be committed in 13 different ways, but in actual practice only three types of balks are common: the pitcher checks himself illegally, breaking his delivery when he is already committed to the pitch; he fails to come to a dead stop while bringing his hands down from the stretch; or the ball slips out of his hand while his foot is on the rubber.

16 ●

The late Tommy Holmes, a baseball writer, used to say that every fan should be presented with a copy of the balk rule on entering the park. That would help, although the rule itself is no model of clarity. Umpires, in calling balks, tend to rely more on custom and experience than on the fine print.

BALL. Called by many other names, including horsehide, apple, onion, pill, pea, sphere, and agate. The rules state that the ball must be a sphere formed by yarn wound around a small core of cork and rubber that is then covered with two strips of white horsehide tightly stitched together. It must weigh not less than 5 or more than 5¼ ounces and measure not less than 9 or more than 9¼ inches all the way around.

Suspicions that baseballs started to be made out of different materials, making for a livelier ball, have been common since 1919, when a marked increase in distance hitting was first noticed. In 1920–1923 almost three times as many home runs were hit in the major leagues as in 1916–1919. The rate kept going up until it leveled off in the 1950s, but baseball officials have never admitted to any change in the composition of the ball.

A core of cork mixed with rubber is covered with a layer of black rubber and a layer of red rubber, and then wound with 121 yards of rough blue-gray wool, 45 yards of white wool, 53 yards of fine blue-gray wool, and 150 yards of fine white cotton. After all this is coated with rubber cement, the cover is sewn by hand—two figure-8-shaped pieces of white horsehide are joined by 108 double stitches of red thread.

Balls used in the two leagues are identical except that each has the signature of its own league president stamped on the cover. A. G. Spalding & Brothers was the exclusive manufacturer of major-league baseballs from the time the leagues began until 1976, when the contract was awarded to the Rawlings Company.

Production costs have risen so sharply in recent years that most of the baseballs used in the major leagues are manufactured in Haiti.

In 1965 it was claimed that the Chicago White Sox stored a number of balls in a cold spot before using them in a game. The purpose of the freezing was to deaden the baseballs and keep them from being hit for long distances. This was believed helpful to the White Sox, a team with little hitting ability and a lot of pitching. The charge was denied by Chicago and never proved by the accusers, but if the White Sox did, indeed, try such shenanigans, it did them no good. They still failed to win the American League pennant.

BALL HAWK. An outfielder, especially one who is very fast and good at chasing down fly balls—and catching them.

BALLS AND STRIKES. A pitch outside a prescribed zone is called a ball, four of which allow the batter to move to first base. A pitch that passes through the zone without being hit is a strike, as is any pitch swung at and missed, a pitch fouled with less than two strikes, or a pitch bunted foul no matter what the count. Three strikes make an out.

The umpire behind the plate is the unquestioned judge (in theory, not in practice) of whether a pitch is a ball or a strike. He keeps track of how many balls and strikes a batter has by means of an indicator, a pocket-sized scoreboard with dials for balls, strikes, and outs.

In announcing the count (number of balls and strikes a batter has), it is proper to give the balls first, the strikes second. So a count of three and two means three balls and two strikes.

BALTIMORE ORIOLES. If one word sums up the history of the Orioles, it is pitching. From their 1966 world championship to the start of the 1980s, the Orioles boasted 20-game-winning pitchers who kept them in contention almost every year.

The Orioles' astonishing sweep of the Dodgers in the 1966 World Series should have served as an omen that the O's were establishing a pitching dynasty. In that Series young hurlers Jim Palmer, Wally Bunker, and Dave McNally helped hold the Dodgers to two runs in four games.

From 1970 through 1980 the Orioles had 19 pitchers who won 20 games or more, including three in their world championship year of 1970, and four (Palmer, McNally, Mike Cuellar, and Pat Dobson) the following season, when they won the pennant.

There was no sign in the Orioles' early history that the team would establish any sort of dynasty. Originating in Milwaukee in 1901 and becoming the St. Louis Browns in 1902, the franchise finished in the first division only 12 times and won its only pennant in 1944, a war year when many of the game's stars were in military service.

After the war ended, the team finished in the second division for eight straight years as attendance dropped. Not even the promotional stunts of owner Bill Veeck could save the team. Veeck finally sold out to a Baltimore group, and the club began a new life in Maryland in 1954.

It wasn't until 1960 that the Orioles became a contender. Led by young third baseman Brooks Robinson and the "Baby Birds"

pitching staff that featured Milt Pappas, Steve Barber, and Chuck Estrada, the O's started their rise to respectability. In 1966 a trade that brought Frank Robinson from Cincinnati set into gear the Orioles' drive to the championship.

They have been in the thick of the American League pennant chase most of the time since then, thanks to the managing of Earl Weaver, and, yes, that magnificent pitching.

BANJO HITTER. A weak hitter who seems to lightly strum the ball as one would a banjo. It is a term of disparagement, but any player will say that even a banjo hit is music to his ears.

BANNER DAY. One of baseball's many promotions (others are Camera Day, Old-Timers' Day, Senior Citizens' Day, and Ladies' Day) designed to create spectator participation and increase attendance. Banner Day had its origin with the New York Mets in the old Polo Grounds and came about purely by accident. Fans began carrying signs and banners to the ballpark to cheer their personal heroes, to make known

● *The Orioles, with batting champion Frank Robinson (right) and Brooks Robinson, swept the Dodgers in the 1966 World Series.*

● *Banner Day at the Mets' Shea Stadium in Flushing, New York*

their grievances, to support their favorite team, or simply to show off their cleverness.

They used bed sheets, cardboard, and rolled-up pieces of paper, and at first the slogans were simple statements in crayon, pen, or pencil. Soon the banners evolved into works of art, and the slogans rivaled Madison Avenue advertising campaigns.

Finally the Mets' promotion department decided to run a competition for creator of the best banner, and among the winners were the following banners:

WHO SAYS A GOOD BASEBALL TEAM
HAS TO WIN?

WORLD SERIES RESERVATIONS
ON SALE . . . FOR 1999.

WE'RE IN THE CELLAR
BUT WE'RE NOT IN THE DUMPS.

TO ERROR IS HUMAN,
TO FORGIVE IS A METS FAN.

BARNSTORMING. Taken from the political and theatrical term that originally meant to appear in small country towns, where barns served as gathering places. Baseball teams barnstorm in the spring, playing exhibitions on their way home from training camp, and star players often assemble into barnstorming units in the fall, playing not only in the United States but occasionally on foreign soil as well. The first foreign tour dates back to 1874, when members of the Boston Red Stockings and the Philadelphia Athletics of the National Association went to Ireland and England to play 14 baseball games and 7 cricket matches.

Five years later Frank Bancroft took a barnstorming team to Havana. In 1888 A.G. Spalding gathered a group of 20 players, mostly from the Chicago National League team, and made the first around-the-world baseball tour, playing in such faraway places as New Zealand, Australia, Ceylon, Egypt, Italy, France, England, and Ireland.

In 1908 the Reach All-America team

● *Yankee stars Lou Gehrig (left) and Babe Ruth, with promoter Christy Walsh, were a sight to see wherever they barnstormed.*

made the first tour of Japan, and later there were additional tours to Japan. In 1931 many of the top stars of the day played four games in Japan and drew the staggering total of 250,000 admissions. Soon after that tour the Japanese developed professional teams for the first time. One of the players on the 1931 trip was Lefty O'Doul, who made five more trips to Japan and became the second greatest sports idol in that country, the first being Babe Ruth, who played

on the 18-game Japanese tour headed by Connie Mack in 1934. In 1955 the New York Yankees went to Japan as a unit to play exhibitions, and since then many teams have played there.

Still, it was mainly through the appearance of Babe Ruth and Lefty O'Doul that the Japanese took to the game of baseball to such a degree that today they are as fanatical about the sport as we are in the United States.

BASE. Also called bag, sack, cushion, hassock, and so on. Any of the four objects to be touched or occupied by the runners. Home base is usually called the plate or the dish and is the starting and finishing point of a trip around the bases which results in the scoring of a run. First, second, and third bases are white canvas bags 15 inches square, not less than 3 or more than 5 inches in thickness, filled with soft material, and securely attached to the ground. They differ from home base, which is a 5-sided slab of whitened rubber. It is 12 inches square with two of the corners filled in so that one edge is 17 inches long, two are 8½ inches, and two are 12 inches. It is set in the ground so that the 17-inch edge faces the pitcher. All bases, including home base, are in fair territory, and the bases are 90 feet apart in the counterclockwise order in which they are to be run.

BASEBALL CARDS. Baseball cards have been around almost as long as baseball, appearing as early as the 1880s in cigarette and tobacco packages. Following the first World War candy manufacturers

● *Baseball cards go a long way back, including the Honus Wagner card valued as high as $15,000. Note that the card manufacturer couldn't spell Pittsburgh.*

WAGNER, PITTSBURG

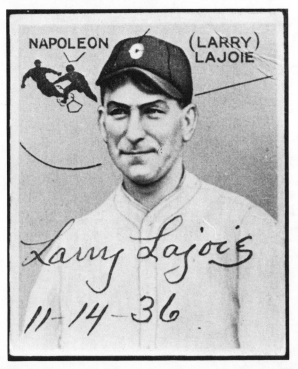

used them to lure purchasers of such goodies as caramels, toffee, mints, and milk cocoa.

By the 1930s the chewing gum companies began packaging pictures of the stars with biographical data or playing tips on the back side.

From the beginning, collecting cards has been a favorite hobby of countless Americans of all ages. Collectors now assemble at conventions, auctions, and club meetings, and are kept up-to-date on what's available through books, magazines, and newsletters. Aside from deriving pleasure from sorting, trading, and assembling, collectors find monetary rewards for a particular, rare card.

Although in modern times Topps chewing gum has been dominant in the manufacture of bubble gum cards, other companies have entered the market, and today's collector can now shop for the gum that offers the most and best cards for the money.

0201–Carroll, COPYRIGHTED, 1887.
Left Field,
Washington

.0178.–Hines. COPYRIGHTED, 1887.
Centre Field
Washington.

.0185–Shoch, COPYRIGHTED, 1887.
Right Field,
Washington.

0171–Kreig, COPYRIGHTED, 1887.
First Base,
Washington.

.0200–Carroll, COPYRIGHTED, 1887.
Left Field,
Washington.

.0193. Donnelly. COPYRIGHTED, 1887.
Third Base.
Washington.

● *This is an artist's rendering of "The Second Great Match Game for the Championship," played in Phila-delphia in 1866. The Philadelphia Athletics defeated the Brooklyn Atlantics, 31–12.*

BASEBALL ORIGINS. As far as organized baseball is concerned, Abner Doubleday is the father of the game. It may well be, however, that one Alexander J. Cartwright dreamed up the sport as we know it and that baseball is keeping alive a myth by crediting Doubleday.

During the Depression of the 1930s the major leagues, trying to stir up lagging interest in the game, came on a 30-year-old report by A.G. Mills, who had been commissioned to look into the origin of baseball. Mills stated, without a particle of proof, that baseball had been invented in 1839 in Cooperstown, New York, by Doubleday, a West Point cadet who later became a Union gen-

eral as well as a close friend of Mills. The major leagues seized on the report, set up a centennial celebration for 1939, and made Cooperstown the site of an official baseball museum and Hall of Fame.

Most baseball historians consider the Mills report a work of fiction, preferring to believe that the sport evolved from old English games, notably rounders, and that Cartwright should have been given credit for formalizing it. Cartwright, a surveyor, laid out the field with the bases 90 feet apart and drew up rules (including three strikes and three outs) for the first game played between organized teams, in Hoboken, New Jersey, in 1846.

BASELINES. The boundary lines within which a base runner must keep when running between the bases. The baselines are not the foul lines and run, in fact, along the foul lines three feet away on either side. Whether or not a runner has stayed within the boundary of the baseline is a source of many heated disputes between players and umpires because, since the action is so fast, the decision is up to the umpire, who has the last word.

BASE ON BALLS. When a batter is allowed to go to first base after receiving four pitches outside the strike zone. Also called a walk. This is the play that defensive managers detest more than any other in baseball because there is no defense against a base on balls—the batter is given a free ticket to a base. Enough free tickets will soon prove to be very damaging.

Frank Frisch was a player and manager turned radio broadcaster for the New York Giants, and not a day would pass that he would not deplore the base on balls. "Oh, those bases on balls" became a Frank Frisch trademark.

The record for receiving most bases on balls in a single season is 170 by Babe Ruth in 1923. The National League record is 148, shared by Eddie Stanky of the Brooklyn Dodgers in 1945 and Jim Wynn of the Houston Astros in 1969. Ruth's record was based on pitchers' fears of his great ability as a hitter, while Stanky's was a tribute to his ability to distract pitchers into throwing balls. He did this by constantly fouling pitches that would have been strikes and by moving around and crouching in the batter's box so that he was a difficult target.

At the time when Stanky was the unchallenged king of the base on balls, Andrei Gromyko was the Russian ambassador to the United Nations, and he occasionally walked out of UN meetings to display his displeasure over the proceedings. This caused one sportswriter to tag Stanky with the nickname Gromyko, and the name stuck.

BASE RUNNER. A player of the team at bat who has finished his turn at bat, reached a base, and has not yet scored or been put out.

BASES LOADED. When first, second, and third bases are all occupied by runners, which is the maximum. Also called bases full, bags bulging, and the ducks are on the pond.

BAT. A smooth, rounded stick not more than 2¾ inches in diameter at its thickest part and not more than 42 inches long. The rules state that it must be one piece of solid wood or formed from a block of wood consisting of two or more pieces of wood bonded together with an adhesive in such a way that the grain direction of all pieces is essentially the same as the length of the bat. Any such laminated bat must contain only wood or adhesive, except for a clear finish.

Bat nicknames have survived long usage; some of the more enduring ones are lumber, wood, wand, willow, war club, stick, hickory. A bat is still called the hickory because it used to be made of that hardwood, although white ash has long since proved more satisfactory.

Thanks to Babe Ruth, bats are much lighter than they were in the days when Babe himself swung a 54-ounce club. Other hitters, going for distance to keep up with Ruth, found they couldn't get the bat around fast enough.

The heaviest bat now used is the 36-ounce model, and only a few, like the Pirates' Dave Parker and Willie Stargell, use it. The average today, according to the Louisville Slugger people, is 33 ounces, and here is how some of the leading hitters weigh in: Carl Yastrzemski, 31–32; Johnny Bench and Dave Kingman, 32; Mike Schmidt, 33–34; Reggie Jackson, 34; and George Foster, 35.

Most professional bats are made by Hillerich & Bradsby. Their Louisville Slugger, in production since 1894, is still the favorite big-league bat. It comes in any number of models, and most players have bats manufactured to their own specifications, so that each player has his own bat model almost from the time he first joins a major-league team.

There is a legend that if a player hits the ball on the trademark of the bat, the bat will break, but that story was born on the sandlots and is not true. During the 1958 World Series, Hank Aaron of the Milwaukee Braves came to bat and New York Yankee catcher Yogi Berra noticed that the trademark was down.

"Hank," Yogi said, "you'd better turn the trademark around so you can read it, otherwise you'll break your bat."

"Yogi," Aaron replied, "I came up here to hit, not to read."

● *Joe Carrieri was batboy for six world championship Yankee teams. Today he's a lawyer.*

Teams also employ ballboys (and ballgirls) who gather up foul balls and supply the umpire with the game's baseballs. A ballboy does not get to go out of town with the team and does not work in close association with the players, but he can work his way up from ballboy to batboy.

BAT AROUND. When all nine batters of one team come to bat in the same inning before there are three outs.

BATBOY. A young man, usually a teenager, who assists a team by handing each player his bat, picking up the bat after the player has hit, and generally caring for and keeping equipment neat and tidy during a game. It is a job that boys want because they get to rub shoulders with their heroes, the players, and are usually on a first-name basis with them.

Batboys are paid a small fee by the team and depend on tips from the players for additional income. Another attraction is the opportunity to make one road trip with the team.

BATTER. An offensive player who takes his position in the batter's box for purposes of hitting the ball. Traditionally, play is in progress when the home-plate umpire shouts, "Batter up!"

BATTER'S BOX. The area within which the batter stands during his time at bat. It is a rectangle six feet long and four feet wide, and the batter must keep both feet in the box at all times when he is hitting.

BATTERY. The pitcher and the catcher. The name has a military origin and dates back to Civil War days when a battery was a group of cannons. Just as the cannons did, the pitcher and catcher start all of the fireworks in a baseball game.

BATTING AVERAGE. A way of measuring a player's batting ability. It is the number of hits he has made divided by his official times at bat and carried to three decimal places. The batting average is an outgrowth of the box score, first kept by Henry Chadwick, the pioneer of all baseball writers, in 1853.

At present .300 (3 hits for every 10 times at bat) is considered an excellent batting average. A .400 average is considered phenomenal. In modern times (since 1900) there have been just eight players who batted .400 or higher for a full season, including Ty Cobb of the Detroit Tigers and Rogers Hornsby of the St. Louis Cardinals, who

Batting Champions

NATIONAL LEAGUE

Year	Player, Club	Avg.	Year	Player, Club	Avg.
1900	Honus Wagner, Pittsburgh Pirates	.380	1942	Ernie Lombardi, Boston Braves	.330
1901	Jesse Burkett, St. Louis Cardinals	.382	1943	Stan Musial, St. Louis Cardinals	.330
1902	C.H. Beaumont, Pittsburgh Pirates	.357	1944	Dixie Walker, Brooklyn Dodgers	.357
1903	Honus Wagner, Pittsburgh Pirates	.355	1945	Phil Cavaretta, Chicago Cubs	.355
1904	Honus Wagner, Pittsburgh Pirates	.349	1946	Stan Musial, St. Louis Cardinals	.365
1905	J. Seymour Bentley, Cincinnati Reds	.377	1947	Harry Walker, St. L. Cardinals– Phila. Phillies	.363
1906	Honus Wagner, Pittsburgh Pirates	.339	1948	Stan Musial, St. Louis Cardinals	.376
1907	Honus Wagner, Pittsburgh Pirates	.350	1949	Jackie Robinson, Brooklyn Dodgers	.342
1908	Honus Wagner, Pittsburgh Pirates	.354	1950	Stan Musial, St. Louis Cardinals	.346
1909	Honus Wagner, Pittsburgh Pirates	.339	1951	Stan Musial, St. Louis Cardinals	.355
1910	Sherwood Magee, Philadelphia Phillies	.331	1952	Stan Musial, St. Louis Cardinals	.336
1911	Honus Wagner, Pittsburgh Pirates	.334	1953	Carl Furillo, Brooklyn Dodgers	.344
1912	Heinie Zimmerman, Chicago Cubs	.372	1954	Willie Mays, New York Giants	.345
1913	Jake Daubert, Brooklyn Dodgers	.350	1955	Richie Ashburn, Philadelphia Phillies	.338
1914	Jake Daubert, Brooklyn Dodgers	.329	1956	Hank Aaron, Milwaukee Braves	.328
1915	Larry Doyle, New York Giants	.320	1957	Stan Musial, St. Louis Cardinals	.351
1916	Hal Chase, Cincinnati Reds	.339	1958	Richie Ashburn, Philadelphia Phillies	.350
1917	Edd Roush, Cincinnati Reds	.341	1959	Hank Aaron, Milwaukee Braves	.328
1918	Zach Wheat, Brooklyn Dodgers	.335	1960	Dick Groat, Pittsburgh Pirates	.325
1919	Edd Roush, Cincinnati Reds	.321	1961	Roberto Clemente, Pittsburgh Pirates	.351
1920	Rogers Hornsby, St. Louis Cardinals	.370	1962	Tommy Davis, Los Angeles Dodgers	.346
1921	Rogers Hornsby, St. Louis Cardinals	.397	1963	Tommy Davis, Los Angeles Dodgers	.326
1922	Rogers Hornsby, St. Louis Cardinals	.401	1964	Roberto Clemente, Pittsburgh Pirates	.339
1923	Rogers Hornsby, St. Louis Cardinals	.384	1965	Roberto Clemente, Pittsburgh Pirates	.329
1924	Rogers Hornsby, St. Louis Cardinals	.424	1966	Matty Alou, Pittsburgh Pirates	.342
1925	Rogers Hornsby, St. Louis Cardinals	.403	1967	Roberto Clemente, Pittsburgh Pirates	.357
1926	Bubbles Hargrave, Cincinnati Reds	.353	1968	Pete Rose, Cincinnati Reds	.335
1927	Paul Waner, Pittsburgh Pirates	.380	1969	Pete Rose, Cincinnati Reds	.348
1928	Rogers Hornsby, Boston Braves	.387	1970	Rico Carty, Atlanta Braves	.366
1929	Lefty O'Doul, Philadelphia Phillies	.398	1971	Joe Torre, St. Louis Cardinals	.363
1930	Bill Terry, New York Giants	.401	1972	Billy Williams, Chicago Cubs	.333
1931	Chick Hafey, St. Louis Cardinals	.349	1973	Pete Rose, Cincinnati Reds	.338
1932	Lefty O'Doul, Brooklyn Dodgers	.368	1974	Ralph Garr, Atlanta Braves	.353
1933	Chuck Klein, Philadelphia Phillies	.368	1975	Bill Madlock, Chicago Cubs	.354
1934	Paul Waner, Pittsburgh Pirates	.362	1976	Bill Madlock, Chicago Cubs	.339
1935	Arky Vaughan, Pittsburgh Pirates	.385	1977	Dave Parker, Pittsburgh Pirates	.338
1936	Paul Waner, Pittsburgh Pirates	.373	1978	Dave Parker, Pittsburgh Pirates	.334
1937	Joe Medwick, St. Louis Cardinals	.374	1979	Keith Hernandez, St. Louis Cardinals	.344
1938	Ernie Lombardi, Cincinnati Reds	.342	1980	Bill Buckner, Chicago Cubs	.324
1939	Johnny Mize, St. Louis Cardinals	.349	1981	Bill Madlock, Pittsburgh Pirates	.341
1940	Debs Garms, Pittsburgh Pirates	.355			
1941	Pete Reiser, Brooklyn Dodgers	.343			

each did it three times, and George Sisler of the St. Louis Browns, who did it twice. The last player in the major leagues to hit .400 was Ted Williams of the Boston Red Sox, who batted .406 in 1941. The last player in the National League to hit .400 was Bill Terry of the New York Giants, who batted .401 in 1930.

The highest batting average in modern times for a single season was .424 by Hornsby in 1924 (536 at-bats, 227 hits). The highest batting average for an entire career was by Cobb, who batted a remarkable .367 for 24 years—covering 3,033 games and including a record 4,191 hits in 11,429 at-bats.

Batting Champions

AMERICAN LEAGUE

Year	Player, Club	Avg.	Year	Player, Club	Avg.
1901	Napoleon Lajoie, Philadelphia Athletics	.422	1941	Ted Williams, Boston Red Sox	.406
1902	Ed Delahanty, Washington Senators	.376	1942	Ted Williams, Boston Red Sox	.356
1903	Napoleon Lajoie, Cleveland Indians	.355	1943	Luke Appling, Chicago White Sox	.328
1904	Napoleon Lajoie, Cleveland Indians	.381	1944	Lou Boudreau, Cleveland Indians	.327
1905·	Elmer Flick, Cleveland Indians	.306	1945	Snuffy Stirnweiss, New York Yankees	.309
1906	George Stone, St. Louis Browns	.358	1946	Mickey Vernon, Washington Senators	.353
1907	Ty Cobb, Detroit Tigers	.350	1947	Ted Williams, Boston Red Sox	.343
1908	Ty Cobb, Detroit Tigers	.324	1948	Ted Williams, Boston Red Sox	.369
1909	Ty Cobb, Detroit Tigers	.377	1949	George Kell, Detroit Tigers	.343
1910	Ty Cobb, Detroit Tigers	.385	1950	Billy Goodman, Boston Red Sox	.354
1911	Ty Cobb, Detroit Tigers	.420	1951	Ferris Fain, Philadelphia Athletics	.344
1912	Ty Cobb, Detroit Tigers	.410	1952	Ferris Fain, Philadelphia Athletics	.327
1913	Ty Cobb, Detroit Tigers	.390	1953	Mickey Vernon, Washington Senators	.337
1914	Ty Cobb, Detroit Tigers	.368	1954	Bobby Avila, Cleveland Indians	.341
1915	Ty Cobb, Detroit Tigers	.370	1955	Al Kaline, Detroit Tigers	.340
1916	Tris Speaker, Cleveland Indians	.386	1956	Mickey Mantle, New York Yankees	.353
1917	Ty Cobb, Detroit Tigers	.383	1957	Ted Williams, Boston Red Sox	.388
1918	Ty Cobb, Detroit Tigers	.382	1958	Ted Williams, Boston Red Sox	.328
1919	Ty Cobb, Detroit Tigers	.384	1959	Harvey Kuenn, Detroit Tigers	.353
1920	George Sisler, St. Louis Browns	.407	1960	Pete Runnels, Boston Red Sox	.320
1921	Harry Heilmann, Detroit Tigers	.393	1961	Norm Cash, Detroit Tigers	.361
1922	George Sisler, St. Louis Browns	.420	1962	Pete Runnels, Boston Red Sox	.326
1923	Harry Heilmann, Detroit Tigers	.398	1963	Carl Yastrzemski, Boston Red Sox	.321
1924	Babe Ruth, New York Yankees	.378	1964	Tony Oliva, Minnesota Twins	.323
1925	Harry Heilmann, Detroit Tigers	.393	1965	Tony Oliva, Minnesota Twins	.321
1926	Heinie Manush, Detroit Tigers	.377	1966	Frank Robinson, Baltimore Orioles	.316
1927	Harry Heilmann, Detroit Tigers	.398	1967	Carl Yastrzemski, Boston Red Sox	.326
1928	Goose Goslin, Washington Senators	.379	1968	Carl Yastrzemski, Boston Red Sox	.301
1929	Lew Fonseca, Cleveland Indians,	.369	1969	Rod Carew, Minnesota Twins	.332
1930	Al Simmons, Philadelphia Athletics	.381	1970	Alex Johnson, California Angels	.329
1931	Al Simmons, Philadelphia Athletics	.390	1971	Tony Oliva, Minnesota Twins	.337
1932	David Alexander, Detroit Tigers– Boston Red Sox	.367	1972	Rod Carew, Minnesota Twins	.318
1933	Jimmie Foxx, Philadelphia Athletics	.356	1973	Red Carew, Minnesota Twins	.350
1934	Lou Gehrig, New York Yankees	.365	1974	Rod Carew, Minnesota Twins	.364
1935	Buddy Myer, Washington Senators	.349	1975	Rod Carew, Minnesota Twins	.359
1936	Luke Appling, Chicago White Sox	.388	1976	George Brett, Kansas City Royals	.333
1937	Charlie Gehringer, Detroit Tigers	.371	1977	Rod Carew, Minnesota Twins	.388
1938	Jimmie Foxx, Boston Red Sox	.349	1978	Rod Carew, Minnesota Twins	.333
1939	Joe DiMaggio, New York Yankees	.381	1979	Fred Lynn, Boston Red Sox	.333
1940	Joe DiMaggio, New York Yankees	.352	1980	George Brett, Kansas City Royals	.390
			1981	Carney Lansford, Boston Red Sox	.336

• *Cincinnati's Johnny Bench takes his cuts in the cage.*

BATTING CAGE. A metal device on wheels used during batting practice, but not during the game, that keeps balls from rolling behind home plate and going into the stands, where they would, undoubtedly, remain.

BATTING ORDER. The order in which a team must come to bat. Also called the lineup. If a player bats out of turn, deliberately or otherwise, he is out, provided the team in the field realizes the error and appeals to the umpire immediately after the illegal batter has finished his time at bat. The only way the batting order can be changed is by the use of a substitute batter (one not already in the game). Once a player has been substituted for, he is no longer permitted to remain in the game.

The batting order is made out in triplicate by the manager on a form provided by the league. The manager keeps one copy for his use and gives one copy to the opposing manager and another to the umpire just before the start of the game.

Many years ago a team would start with nine players and almost always finish with the same nine men. In recent years baseball has become much more specialized, and use of substitutes has become so widespread that it is rare when a team finishes a game with the same nine men who started it.

BATTING PRACTICE. The players' favorite pastime. A given amount of time, usually an hour, set aside before each game so that hitters can practice hitting. The poor hitters need it the most but get it the least, because most of the time is taken up by the regulars, who are protective of their allotted time.

BEANBALL. A pitch suspected of having been aimed at a batter's head. Pitchers, according to pitchers, never throw beanballs. Quote: "It slipped," or "I was just brushing him back" (throwing close to the batter to keep him from taking a toehold). At times such explanations are regarded with a certain amount of cynicism, especially by batters. In recent years umpires have been empowered to censure a pitcher thought to be deliberately throwing a beanball (whether he connects or not). With the censure comes an automatic $50 fine, and repeated violations can lead to a larger fine, banishment from a game, and suspension from baseball.

In 1920 Carl Mays, a pitcher with the New York Yankees, hit Ray Chapman, a shortstop for the Cleveland Indians, in the head with a pitch. Chapman was rushed to New York's Knickerbocker Hospital, where he died from the blow the following morning. Because it was fatal, this incident has been regarded as the most famous, or infamous, of all the beanings. But there is no evidence that it was intentional.

In the early 1950s Branch Rickey, then president of the Pittsburgh Pirates, instructed all of his players to wear a specially constructed plastic helmet to protect the head when batting. The practice soon became widespread, and now a batter must go to the plate with a protective helmet on.

BEAT OUT. To hit safely by beating an infielder's throw to first base. Most commonly used in connection with a bunt. A player beats out a bunt.

BENCH. Applies not only to the seating facilities reserved for players, substitutes, and other team members in uniform in the dugout, but also to a team's substitutes as a group. Thus the saying, "A team is only as strong as its bench." To bench a player means to remove him from the starting lineup for playing poorly. A player who does not play frequently is said to be riding the bench or a bench-warmer. He is a substitute or utility player, sometimes called a scrub or, in modern jargon, scrubeenie. Frank Torre, when he played for the Milwaukee Braves, used the expression "Vitalis" for a scrub. "Because," as he put it, "he would get only a sixty-second workout." This was inspired by a popular television hair-tonic commercial of the day.

In bygone days a bench-warmer or scrub was a much sneered-at player who rarely got into a game because he was not considered good enough to play. In recent years, with the age of the specialist, the bench has become a very vital part of any team. Casey Stengel, when he managed the Yankees, made popular the use of the bench. He would have almost two offensive teams, one right-handed team to bat against left-handed pitchers and one left-handed hitting team to bat against right-handed pitchers. But certain players, such as Joe DiMaggio, were not replaced by bench-warmers. Stengel also made use of defensive specialists, who made their appearance late in games in which the Yankees had a lead.

In 1954 Dusty Rhodes of the New York Giants gave the bench-warmer added stature. Rhodes rarely started a game, but, used mostly as a pinch-hitter, he batted .341 for the season. In the World Series against Cleveland, Rhodes came off the bench in each of the first three games to deliver important hits and help the Giants sweep the Series. Rhodes's three-run, pinch-hit home run in the tenth inning won the first game, 5–2.

BENCH, JOHNNY. The ball jumped off Johnny Bench's bat with the familiar crack that said "Home run!" It soared toward the left-field seats in Cincinnati's Riverfront Stadium—Bench Country.

And as it disappeared over the fence, Bench took a step toward first base and then jumped in the air, celebrating the shot that put him in the record book. When Bench connected against Montreal on July 15, 1980, it was his 314th homer as a catcher, breaking the mark established by Hall of Famer Yogi Berra.

During the seventies he established himself as the game's most productive hitter, driving in 1,013 runs. Bench also blasted 290 home runs over that period, trailing only Willie Stargell (296) and Reggie Jackson (292).

Bench is the all-time Cincinnati career home-run and RBI leader. After the 1981 season he had 364 homers, becoming twenty-ninth on the all-time list and fourth among active players behind Stargell, Carl Yastrzemski, and Jackson. A 13-time All-Star, he has hit 20 or more homers in 11 different seasons. He had a total of 1,284 RBI's. The only catcher with more for his career was Berra, who drove in 1,430.

● *Many ballplayers wander from team to team, but Johnny Bench found a permanent home in Cincinnati.*

Bench has scored those brilliant batting numbers while playing at one of baseball's most demanding positions. He tied a National League record in 1980, catching 100 games for the thirteenth season in a row. The only other man to accomplish that was Bill Dickey, another Hall of Famer.

Born on December 7, 1947, in Oklahoma City, Bench was just 19 when he caught his first major-league game in 1967. It was the start of an awesome career that has included 3 RBI championships, 2 MVP awards, and 10 consecutive Gold Gloves for his defensive play.

BERRA, YOGI. It was a standard picture, repeated, it seemed, every October. In it Yogi Berra, the squat, square catcher of the New York Yankees, would go leaping into the arms of a pitcher, celebrating still another pennant or world championship.

Berra's career as one of baseball's star catchers is entwined with the Yankee dynasty years—an awesome stretch from 1947 to 1963 when New York played in 14 of a possible 17 Series. He set records for games, at-bats, hits, and singles and played in 30 games in a row without an error. When he retired in 1964, the Yankees made him their manager and he took them into another Series. Berra also managed the New York Mets into the 1973 Series, becoming one of the few men in baseball history to pilot pennant winners in both leagues.

Like his longtime manager, Casey Stengel, Berra became one of America's most recognizable and beloved characters. His occasionally fractured sayings charmed listeners. For example, "If people don't want to come to the ballpark, how are you gonna stop them?" Or, "We made too many wrong mistakes." But there was nothing funny about his performance. He was a quality catcher and one of the best hitters of his time. His 313 career home runs was a

• *The throw comes too late for the Yankees' Yogi Berra to get his man, Washington's Sam Dente, in a 1949 game.*

BLEACHERS. Stands that got their names because they were uncovered, causing the occupants to bleach in the sun.

BLEEDER. A lucky one-base hit, sometimes called a scratch hit. Usually it is a grounder that is hit softly and trickles through the infield, takes a bad hop, or rolls dead in front of a charging infielder.

BONER. A foolish error, known also as a bonehead play, a skull or skuller, or a rock. A classic baseball boner was Fred Merkle's failure to touch second base when a teammate drove in the winning run for the New York Giants late in the 1908 season. Johnny Evers of the Chicago Cubs called for the ball, touched second base, and had Merkle declared out, nullifying the run. The Cubs won the pennant on the last day of the season, and Merkle went down in history as the man responsible for the Giants' not winning it.

Another classic boner was when three Brooklyn Dodgers in the 1920s wound up at third base at the same time after a line drive landed safely in right field. One player thought the ball would be caught, the other two did not, thus the mix-up.

record for catchers until Johnny Bench broke it in 1980. Overall, Berra had 358 homers.

Berra, born on May 12, 1925, in St. Louis, was the American League's Most Valuable Player three times and was named to the All-Star team 15 times. In 1972 he was elected to the Hall of Fame.

BETWEEN THE LINES. The field, foul line to foul line. Players often say, "It's what happens between the lines that counts," meaning that what a player does in the game is what matters, not his off-field activities.

BONUS PLAYER. Modern term for a raw prospect who receives a lot of money for signing. Robin Roberts ($25,000), Al Kaline ($60,000), and Tony Conigliaro ($35,000) are among the few bonus players who made good. A celebrated failure was Paul Pettit, who won one game in his brief career with the Pittsburgh Pirates after he had been sold to them for $100,000 by a Hollywood agent, who kept 10 percent.

The largest bonuses ever paid are said to be the $175,000 the Pirates gave infielder Bob Bailey and the $200,000 the Los Angeles Angels handed to outfielder Rick Reichardt in 1964, which may never be topped. To put an end to the bartering that threatened to drive bonuses to ridiculous heights, in 1965 the major leagues adopted a program of drafting amateur players. The first player drafted was Rick Monday, an outfielder from Arizona State University, who was selected by the Kansas City Athletics. He got $100,000 for signing, but might have received more than twice that amount before the amateur draft.

No matter how much is spent in search of a gem of a player, there are no guarantees. And there is always someone who comes along at a bargain price and makes it as a star. Mickey Mantle, for example, was discovered by Yankee scout Tom Greenwade, who showed up on the Oklahoma sandlots to sign another player and took Mantle for a mere $1,100.

• *Boston's Carl Yastrzemski singles in a 1967 World Series game against the St. Louis Cardinals.*

BOSTON RED SOX. Though the team has had limited success through its history, the Red Sox have provided their adoring fans with some of the most dramatic moments in baseball history.

In 1967 the Red Sox zoomed toward clinching the American League pennant after finishing ninth the year before. On the final day of the season, as a Fenway Park capacity crowd went wild, Jim Lonborg nailed down the team's first pennant in 21 years.

Eight years later Carlton Fisk sent another Fenway crowd into delirium when his home run in the twelfth inning gave the Red Sox a victory over Cincinnati in the sixth game of the World Series. But Boston lost the seventh game.

Since 1920 Boston has won only 3 pennants while finishing last 11 times. At one time, though, the team dominated the league. In 1903 it won the pennant and the first World Series ever played. The Red Sox won the World Series four times between 1912 and 1918, but made a costly mistake in 1920 when owner Harry Frazee, needing money, sold Babe Ruth to the Yankees. After the Babe left, the Red Sox finished in the second division 15 straight years, while the Yankees won 7 pennants.

But Boston revived in the 1940s as new owner Tom Yawkey developed stars like Bobby Doerr, Dom DiMaggio, and the incomparable Ted Williams. Williams, called by many the best pure hitter the game has ever produced, is the last man to bat .400 in a season (.406 in 1941).

The Red Sox have had their superstars since then, but none as durable and productive as Carl (Yaz) Yastrzemski, who joined the team in 1961 and was still clearing the fences in the early 1980s.

BOTTOM. The second, or home team's, half of an inning.

BOX SCORE. A standardized table showing at a glance the batting order, position of the player, at-bats (ab), runs (r), hits (h), runs batted in (rbi). After the batting summary there is a line score showing the runs made in each inning and the final score. Under the line score there is a listing of errors (E), double plays (DP), left on base (LOB), two-base hits (2B), three-base hits (3B—none in this game), home runs (HR), stolen bases (SB), sacrifices (S). This is followed by a listing of the pitchers that gives: innings pitched (IP), how many hits (H), runs (R), earned runs (ER), bases on balls (BB), and strikeouts (SO). The winning and losing pitchers are indicated by W and L with their won-lost records. The bottom line lists saves, wild pitches (WP), time it took to play the game (T), and attendance (A). The first box score appeared in the New York *Clipper* in 1853.

Seventh Game, 1975 World Series

CINCINNATI

	ab	r	h	rbi
Rose 3b	4	0	2	1
Morgan 2b	4	0	2	1
Bench c	4	1	0	0
Perez 1b	5	1	1	2
Foster lf	4	0	1	0
Concepcion ss	4	0	1	0
Griffey rf	2	2	1	0
Geronimo cf	3	0	0	0
Gullett p	1	0	1	0
Rettenmund ph	1	0	0	0
Billingham p	0	0	0	0
Armbrister ph	0	0	0	0
Carroll p	0	0	0	0
Driessen ph	1	0	0	0
McEnaney p	0	0	0	0
Total	33	4	9	4

BOSTON

	ab	r	h	rbi
Carbo lf	3	1	1	0
Miller lf	0	0	0	0
Beniquez ph	1	0	0	0
Doyle 2b	4	1	1	0
Montgomery ph	1	0	0	0
Yastrzemski 1b	5	1	1	1
Fisk c	3	0	0	0
Lynn cf	2	0	0	0
Petrocelli 3b	3	0	1	1
Evans rf	2	0	0	1
Burleson ss	3	0	0	0
Lee p	3	0	1	0
Moret p	0	0	0	0
Willoughby p	0	0	0	0
Cooper ph	1	0	0	0
Burton p	0	0	0	0
Cleveland p	0	0	0	0
Total	31	3	5	3

```
Cincinnati . . . . . . . . . . . . . . . . . . . . . . . . . . . . . .000 002 101—4
Boston . . . . . . . . . . . . . . . . . . . . . . . . . . . . . . . . .003 000 000—3
```

E—Doyle 2. DP—Cincinnati 1, Boston 2. LOB—Cincinnati 9, Boston 9. 2B—Carbo. HR—Perez (3). SB—Morgan, Griffey. S—Geronimo.

	IP	H	R	ER	BB	SO
Gullett	4	4	3	3	5	5
Billingham	2	1	0	0	2	1
Carroll (W, 1–0)	2	0	0	0	1	1
McEnaney	1	0	0	0	0	0
Lee	6⅓	7	3	3	1	2
Moret	⅓	1	0	0	2	0
Willoughby	1⅓	0	0	0	0	0
Burton (L, 0–1)	⅔	1	1	1	2	0
Cleveland	⅓	0	0	0	1	0

Save—McEnaney (1). WP—Gullett. T—2.52. A—35,205.

BRETT, GEORGE. It was a hot, muggy August night in 1980 in Kansas City, where the summer heat can be oppressive. But instead of worrying about the thermometer, the Royals' fans were on their feet cheering madly as George Brett stood triumphantly on second base with a double.

Finally Brett took off his cap and waved it to the fans, acknowledging their cheers for what had been his fourth hit of the game against Toronto. The hit thrust Brett past the magic .400 mark, a batting average no major leaguer has achieved by season's end in 40 years.

For the next six weeks the Kansas City star would carry on an exciting drive to end up at .400. The Royals were light-years ahead of the other teams in the American League Western Division, and only Brett's quest for .400 maintained the interest of fans everywhere through the stretch of season commonly called the dog days.

Brett fell short, finishing at .390 with 24

• *George Brett: the man who came closest to .400*

home runs and 118 runs batted in for his magic season. Five more hits—less than one hit per month over the course of the season—would have produced the .400 season. But a thumb injury in September hurt his swing and kept him from making it.

His challenge in 1980 established the fact that he is a constant candidate to hit .400. "He has the tools, the ability to do it," said Charley Lau, the hitting coach Brett credits with his development as a quality batter.

Born on May 15, 1953, in Glen Dale, West Virginia, Brett grew up with dreams of becoming a major leaguer. They were heightened when he sat in the stands at the 1967 World Series and watched his brother Ken, 19 at the time, become the youngest pitcher in Series history. "That clinched it for me," Brett said. "After that, all I could think about was being a ballplayer."

He had become *some* ballplayer. An artist at bat, master of the craft of hitting a baseball, he was the textbook definition of a successful batter—patient, selective, smart, and talented. By 1981 he had won two batting championships, and baseball men said he'd win a few more before he was through.

BROCK, LOU. Of all the one-sided trades in baseball history, the one that brought Lou Brock to the Cardinals from the Cubs in 1964 takes the cake. The Cubs received three players who wound up making no real contributions, while Brock went on to reach the 3,000-hit mark and become baseball's all-time stolen base king.

In 1974 Brock, a native of El Dorado, Arkansas, broke Maury Wills's single-season base-stealing mark with 118, an amazing feat for a man of 35. His career total of 938 topped Ty Cobb's old mark of 892, and he led the National League in stolen bases 9 times.

Brock retired in 1979 with 3,023 hits and a .292 lifetime average.

● *The slide was Lou Brock's trademark.*

BRUSHBACK.   *See* Duster.

BULLPEN.   An area next to the playing field, usually alongside the foul lines, where relief pitchers and other substitutes warm up. The word "bullpen," which is also prison slang for a place of temporary confinement, is of uncertain origin in baseball. Some think it can be traced to the Bull Durham tobacco signs that were posted on the fences of many ballparks in 1909. Featured on the sign was a picture of a gigantic bull, and in many parks relief pitchers warmed up directly in front of it. As far back as 1877, though, bullpen was the name used for a roped-off section of the outfield that served as standing room. The term was used in Civil War days to describe the stockade.

BUNT.   A ball that is not swung at, but intentionally hit with the bat and tapped slowly within the infield. This maneuver is perfected, usually, by speedy runners, because a well-placed bunt is almost always a safe hit. Among those more skilled at the art of bunting for a base hit were Brooklyn Dodger Jackie Robinson, New York Yankee Phil Rizzuto, Los Angeles Dodger Maury Wills, and, more recently, Kansas City Royal and California Angel Freddie Patek.

● *Only 5-foot-5, Fred Patek made the most of the bunt.*

● *The bushes means playing in a minor-league park like this one in Dubuque, Iowa, where the Illinois Central trains are a bonus.*

BUSH. Any league below the majors, but especially a league of very low classification. Bush is also the ballplayers' scornful adjective for any person, thing, or action not meeting with their approval, whether or not it has anything to do with baseball. A player whose conduct or ability is considered not befitting major-league status is called bush, bush league, or a busher. Playing in the minor leagues is also called playing in the bushes.

BUTCHER. A player who is a very poor fielder. He is also said to have a bad glove or bad hands. Such a player was Dick Stuart, a hard hitter for the Pittsburgh Pirates, Boston Red Sox, and Philadelphia Phillies, but one who never dazzled with his defensive work at first base. A Boston sportswriter dubbed him Dr. Strangeglove. Another who had a reputation for being a poor fielder, perhaps without justification, was Chuck Hiller, a second baseman with the San Francisco Giants and New York Mets. His nicknames were Iron Hands, No Hands, and Dr. No.

CALIFORNIA ANGELS. The situation seemed impossible. Nolan Ryan needed 16 strikeouts in his final game of the 1973 season to break Sandy Koufax's record for strikeouts in a season (382). Ryan was tired; he had already gone through 40 games and pitched 315 innings. Could he find enough strength to strike out 16 Minnesota Twins?

Ryan started well, striking out the side in the first inning. Gradually he closed in on the record, but he still needed one more strikeout as the game entered the eleventh inning. With two out, Rich Reese came up. Fastball, strike one. Another fastball, strike two. Finally Ryan fired his hardest pitch of the night, and Reese went down swinging. Ryan had struck out his 383rd batter.

Ryan's achievements were among the few highlights of a team that began life in 1961 when the American League voted to expand to 10 teams and awarded one of two new franchises to a Los Angeles group headed by movie cowboy Gene Autry.

The Angels stunned the baseball world when they finished third in the league in their second year and a zany, much-traveled minor leaguer named Bo Belinsky pitched the team's first no-hitter against the Baltimore Orioles.

After starting out in little Wrigley Field, for the next four years the Angels shared Dodger Stadium in Chavez Ravine with their National League counterparts. In 1966 they moved to nearby Anaheim into their own ballpark, Anaheim Stadium. They changed their name from the Los Angeles Angels to the California Angels. Everyone agreed that it was a more stately name. But it wasn't until 1979 that the Angels, with Rod Carew, MVP Don Baylor, Dan Ford, and Bobby Grich, achieved their first divisional title.

CALLED GAME. A game in which, for any reason, the umpire-in-chief ends play. The most common reason is rain, but games have been called because of snow, fog, and wind. If a game is called before the team trailing has been to bat five times, it is replayed from the beginning. If a game is called after the team trailing has been to bat five times, it is an official game and goes into the records as a shortened game.

CAMPANELLA, ROY. The Los Angeles Coliseum's lights were turned off and all at once the huge ballpark was

● *The Dodgers' Roy Campanella nails the Yankees' Billy Martin at the plate in the 1953 World Series.*

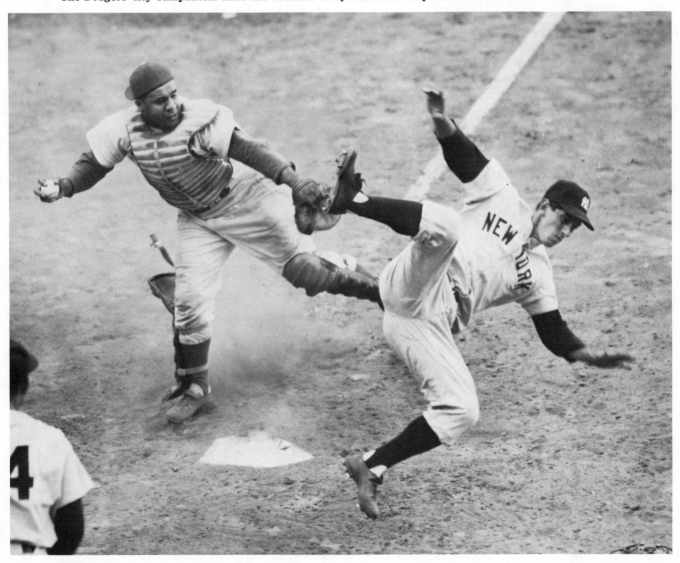

plunged into darkness. Then the fans, 93,103 of them, lit matches and lighters in tribute to one of baseball's immortals. As Roy Campanella was wheeled to home plate, it was one of the most emotional moments in sports history.

The Dodgers and Yankees, longtime World Series rivals, were playing an exhibition game that night to honor Campanella, the Hall of Fame catcher whose career was cut short when he was paralyzed in an automobile accident in the winter of 1958. Campy played 10 seasons with the Dodgers in Brooklyn and appeared in 5 World Series, all of them against the Yankees. He was one of the sturdiest, most dependable catchers of his era.

Born in Philadelphia on November 19, 1921, Campy played his early baseball in the black leagues where he developed his skills. He was an accomplished catcher by 1948 when he came to the Dodgers, one year after Jackie Robinson had been the first black player to perform in the major leagues.

For the next decade Campanella was a feared slugger. He won MVP awards in 1951, 1953, and 1955; led the National League with 142 RBI's in 1953; and was a defensive giant behind the plate, a genius at handling pitchers.

CAN OF CORN. A high fly within easy reach of a fielder.

CAREW, ROD. Rod Carew stepped off third base, measuring his strides, watching the pitcher, studying every move the man on the mound made. Slowly but surely Carew lengthened his lead, growing a bit bolder with each delivery. Finally he was off, dashing down the line, streaking for home plate. As the batter fell away Carew came in flying, sliding across the plate with another Minnesota run.

The year was 1969 and Carew was on his way to the first of his seven American League batting championships. He batted .332 that season, and as deadly as he was at the plate, he was proving almost as destructive on the bases, especially when he was on third base. Carew had 19 stolen bases that season, not that unusual. But 7 of those steals were suicidal dashes down the third-base line that meant runs for Minnesota and a line in the record book for Carew. No American League player has stolen home as frequently in one season as did Carew that season.

But Carew made his mark in baseball as a hitter, not a base stealer. Blessed with a

● *Rod Carew won seven American League batting crowns, including the one in 1977 when he hit .388.*

classic stroke, Carew is a line-drive hitter who sprays the ball all over the diamond. "I could always hit a baseball," he explained. "When I'm hitting, there's nobody in the world who can get me out."

American League pitchers supported that statement. During the seventies Carew batted .343. After his first batting title in 1969, Carew won the crown 6 times in the 7 years 1972–1978. His best season was 1977, when he batted .388 and won the American League's Most Valuable Player award.

In 1979 he became a California Angel and continued his productive career, hitting .331 in 1980 and .305 in 1981.

Carew was born on October 1, 1945, on a train traveling between Gatun and Panama City in the Panama Canal Zone. His family moved to New York City when Rod was a teenager, and Twins scout Herb Stein discovered him. He came to the majors as a second baseman and switched to first in 1975, making the transfer as smoothly as he strokes baseballs.

● *Steve Carlton talks only with his arm.*

CARLTON, STEVE. The cheers began slowly but built quickly into a wall of sound. The fans in St. Louis' Busch Stadium were saluting a unique accomplishment by a visiting player. Steve Carlton of the Philadelphia Phillies had just struck out Tony Scott—the 2,933rd batter Carlton had sent back to the dugout, dragging his bat behind him. No left-hander in the history of baseball had ever struck out more hitters.

On the mound Carlton did nothing to acknowledge the moment. There was no wave of the cap to the crowd, no sign of emotion, not even a smile. Carlton merely went to work on the next Cardinal batter, biting the corners of the plate with his curve, slipping past his slider, exploding his fastball. It was just another day at the office for the efficient southpaw who is so private a person that he avoids interviews.

When he pitched the deciding victory in Philadelphia's 1980 World Series triumph over Kansas City, he sipped his celebration champagne in the trainer's room, avoiding the traditional clubhouse turmoil.

Carlton, who was born in Miami on December 22, 1944, began his big-league career with the Cardinals in 1965. He was a 20-game winner in 1971. He joined the Phillies in 1972, winning 27 games that year, and has had three other 20-victory seasons since then. In 1980, besides winning 24 games, Carlton pitched his sixth career one-hitter and earned a record-tying third Cy Young Award.

• *All the world knew Charles Dillon Stengel simply as Casey.*

CASEY. The well-known nickname of the late Charles Dillon Stengel, famed manager of the Brooklyn Dodgers, Boston Braves, New York Yankees, and New York Mets. He holds the record of having won 10 American League pennants and 7 world championships in 12 years, and was the only manager to have won 5 world championships in a row (1949 to 1953, with the Yankees). Along with Babe Ruth, Casey was regarded as baseball's greatest ambassador, and he had spent more than 50 years in the game when he retired from the Mets in 1965 after his seventy-fifth birthday. His nickname stems from the fact that he came from Kansas City (KC), Missouri.

"CASEY AT THE BAT." The foremost ballad of baseball, written in 1888 by Ernest L. Thayer and made popular by De Wolf Hopper.

CASTOFF. A discarded player, often one who makes a major comeback with another team. Among outstanding examples of castoffs are Dixie Walker, Lew Burdette, and John Mayberry. Walker could not suc-

ceed with the Yankees, White Sox, and Tigers, but when he was picked up by the Brooklyn Dodgers, for whom he played nine seasons, he won the National League batting title in 1944 with a .357 average and finished with a lifetime batting average of .306. He became such a great favorite with Brooklyn fans that he got to be known as the Peepul's Cherce.

Burdette was a minor leaguer in the Yankee farm system when they traded him to the Braves, who then played in Boston. Burdette went on to win 173 games in 11 seasons with the Braves, and in the 1957 World Series he beat the Yankees three times, including two shutouts.

Mayberry was traded by the Houston Astros to the Kansas City Royals when he was just 21, and he became a star in the American League, once given the chance to play. In his first four seasons he drove in 100 or more runs three times.

CATCH. When a fielder gets firm possession in his hand or glove of a ball in flight and holds it. If a fielder has made the catch and drops the ball while in the act of throwing, the ball is considered to have been caught. In establishing that a catch was made, a fielder must hold the ball long enough to prove that he has complete control of it and that his release of the ball is voluntary and intentional.

CATCHER. The fielder who squats behind the plate to receive the pitch. Included among the catcher's special equipment are a mask made of metal, shin guards, and a padded chest protector. Until 1966 the rules permitted the catcher to be the only man on the team who could wear a glove of unlimited size, shape, or weight, the only restriction being that it be made of leather. However, some players took advantage of this rule, using oversized gloves—usually for the purpose of catching the unpredicta-

• *Carlton Fisk, with Chicago White Sox teammate Ed Farmer, is the picture-book catcher.*

ble knuckleball—so the rule was changed. In 1966 the size of the catcher's glove was restricted to no more than 38 inches all the way around and no more than 15½ inches from top to bottom.

The catcher gives signals to the pitcher, telling him what pitch to throw. But the pitcher can disagree, by shaking his head, and then the catcher will ask for another pitch. (*See also* Signals.)

CATCHER'S BOX. Where the catcher stands until the pitcher delivers the ball. He may stay anywhere in the area, which is 8 feet long and 43 inches wide, as long as he does not interfere with the batter.

CATCHER'S INTERFERENCE. Interference by the catcher with the batter, for which the batter goes to first base and is not charged with a time at bat and the catcher is charged with an error. Sometimes called a catcher's balk. If a base runner

attempts to steal at the time the catcher interferes with the batter, the runner is awarded the stolen base (even if he is tagged out), and the batter is still awarded first base.

CENTER FIELD. The outfield territory beyond second base and between that usually covered by the right and left fielders. The outfielder who covers center field is called the center fielder. He is usually the fastest and best of the three outfielders. Among the outstanding center fielders have been Tris Speaker of the Cleveland Indians, Terry Moore of the St. Louis Cardinals, Joe DiMaggio of the New York Yankees, Duke Snider of the Brooklyn Dodgers, Willie Mays of the San Francisco Giants, Mickey Mantle of the Yankees, and Paul Blair of the Baltimore Orioles.

CHANCE. Any opportunity to field a ball with the possibility of making or helping to make a putout. Traditionally, the first baseman accepts the most chances, since most infield outs end with him. The record for the most chances accepted in a season was set by a first baseman, John Donahue of the Chicago White Sox, who had 1,986 chances in 1907; the record for most chances in a nine-inning game is 22, shared by many first basemen.

CHANGE OF PACE. Also called changeup, change, letup, or pulling the string. A slowball usually thrown after a fastball, with the same motion as the fastball, in order to catch the batter off stride. A slow curveball can also be used as a change of pace after a fast curveball. The forkball, palmball, and slip pitch are all examples of pitches used as changes of pace.

CHARITY HOP. The last, long hop taken by some groundballs, making them easy to field.

CHICAGO CUBS.

CHICAGO CUBS. No other franchise can look back on a history as checkered with early triumphs and later failures as the Chicago Cubs.

From the time Al Spalding pitched and managed the White Stockings (they became the Cubs in 1900) to a pennant in the first National League race in 1876 through the next 70 years, Chicago won 16 league titles, the third-highest total among National League teams. But since 1945 no pennant flag has flown above the ivy-covered walls of Wrigley Field.

Many of the most celebrated Cubs were part of the team's early success. Five-time batting champ Cap Anson managed three winners in the 1880s. Frank Chance led the team to the best regular-season record in major-league history (116-36) in 1906 and World Series victories the next two seasons. Chance is most often remembered as the player who, along with Joe Tinker and John Evers, formed a Cub double-play combina-

tion that was immortalized in verse as Tinker-to-Evers-to-Chance.

Rogers Hornsby, who batted .380 in 1929; Hack Wilson, who in 1930 had a league record 56 homers and 190 runs batted in; and Gabby Hartnett, whose dramatic final-week homer sparked the Cubs to the 1938 pennant, were Cub legends. After they departed, the team fell on hard times.

Owner Phil Wrigley, the chewing-gum king, kept his vow that there would be no night baseball in his park. So the oldest stadium in the National League remains the only one in baseball not equipped with lights. Critics have suggested that the demands of playing day after day in the grueling summer sun and the luxury of having nights off have wilted some Cub contenders down the stretch.

Whatever the reasons, Chicago's failure and Wrigley's frustration were so great that the owner, tired of hiring and firing managers, put the team into the hands of a rotating set of coaches from 1961 to 1965. That, too, was no help.

The wait for another title has been so long that Ernie Banks, the man known as Mr. Cub after spending 18 years in that uniform, hit 512 career home runs and won Gold Gloves at shortstop and first base, but never got to play in a World Series.

● *Mr. Cub: Ernie Banks*

CHICAGO WHITE SOX.

CHICAGO WHITE SOX. There have been glorious moments in the history of the Chicago White Sox. In 1906 they won the American League pennant and went on to win the World Series against their hated crosstown rival, the Cubs. In 1917 they won another world championship, beating the Giants in six games despite their nickname the Hitless Wonders because they had a team batting average of .228.

But the focus of any story written about the White Sox will always be about how they became known as the Black Sox after purposely losing the 1919 World Series to the underdog Cincinnati Reds.

It was an exceptional White Sox team that won the American League pennant in 1919. It had two 20-game winners in Eddie Cicotte and Claude Williams, and a magnificent hitter in Shoeless Joe Jackson. But something went wrong. The Reds battered Cicotte, 9–1, in the first game. One team had to win 5 out of 9 games, and the Reds clinched the Series, 5 games to 3.

Rumors spread quickly that the Series had been fixed, and in 1920 American League president Ban Johnson revealed the full details of an alleged conspiracy among eight Chicago players and gamblers. Although the eight players were never found guilty in the courts, Baseball Commissioner Kenesaw Mountain Landis banned them, including Jackson, Cicotte, and Williams, from baseball for life.

It took years for the White Sox to recover. It wasn't until 1936 that they got out of the second division. And it wasn't until 40 years later, in 1959, that the White Sox made it back to the World Series, losing to the Los Angeles Dodgers in six games.

That 1959 team had some fine players, including American League MVP Nellie Fox at second base, major-league stolen base king Luis Aparicio at short, and a pitching staff that included Hall of Famer Early Wynn.

The White Sox have not been back in the World Series since then, coming close several times in the 1960s but always falling short.

CHOKE. To grip a bat several inches up from the end. It is done deliberately when a batter wants to bunt the ball. It also means to fail in a critical situation, or to let your emotions get the better of you. So, under pressure, a player may choke, choke up, get the apple, get the lump, get the olive, get tight.

CINCINNATI REDS. In a sense baseball started in Cincinnati, which became the home of the sport's first all-professional team in 1869. The Red Stockings, who won 130 games over two seasons before suffering their first loss, and became the Redlegs or Reds in 1876, were involved in a series of baseball firsts.

Cincinnati, whose home opener traditionally starts each National League season, was the first franchise to play a night game (May 24, 1935, against Philadelphia at Crosley Field), to have a Ladies' Day, to option a player, to travel by air, and to play a televised game (August 26, 1939, in Brooklyn).

With pitchers Bucky Walters and Paul Derringer leading the way, Cincinnati won back-to-back pennants in 1939 and 1940 and, after being swept by the Yankees in the 1939 World Series, bounced back to beat the Tigers in seven games the following year. That was actually the Reds' second World Series victory; their first—in 1919 over the Chicago "Black Sox"—was tarnished by the gambling scandal that blackened the game.

Southpaw Johnny Vander Meer left his mark in 1938 when he pitched two no-hit games in a row against Boston and Brooklyn.

• *Pete Rose (14) and his teammates celebrate winning the 1975 World Series over the Red Sox.*

The Reds rode the bats of Frank Robinson and Vada Pinson to a 1961 pennant, but after dropping that Series to the Yankees, the club was forced to rebuild. When it did, the result was a Big Red Machine that dominated baseball in the 1970s under the direction of Sparky Anderson.

Fueled by such great hitters as Joe Morgan, Pete Rose, Ken Griffey, Johnny Bench (who has hit more homers than any other catcher in history), and Tony Perez, the Reds won pennants in 1970 and 1972 and world championships in 1975 and 1976. The 1975 seven-game struggle against the Red Sox is remembered as perhaps the greatest Series in history.

CIRCUIT. A home run (a circuit clout) or a league (senior circuit for National League, junior circuit for American League).

CIRCUS CATCH. A spectacular catch of a fly ball, usually by an outfielder.

CLEAN-UP BATTER. The fourth position in the batting order, so called because it is usually manned by a slugger, who regularly drives in any runners who may have reached base ahead of him, thus cleaning the bases. It used to be customary for a manager to bat his best hitter in the clean-up position, but in recent years the trend has been to bat the best hitter third because of the possibility that the third batter will get more times at bat than the clean-up hitter.

CLEMENTE, ROBERTO. It was New Year's Eve, 1972, a time for celebration. But a party was the last thing on Roberto Clemente's mind. He was thinking, instead, of a rescue mission to bring food and supplies to the victims of an earthquake in Managua, Nicaragua.

Clemente, a Pittsburgh Pirate superstar, helped load a rescue plane and took off with it from his native Puerto Rico. But the plane crashed at sea and Clemente's body was never recovered.

It was a devastating loss, especially for the fans who had finally come to appreciate Clemente's vast skills during Pittsburgh's 1971 World Series victory over Baltimore. The Pirate right fielder was brilliant in those seven games, batting .414 and fielding, running, and throwing magnificently.

Clemente won four batting championships in 18 National League seasons and compiled a lifetime average of .317. When he got his 3,000th hit in 1972, the last one of his life, he became only the eleventh player in history to achieve that level.

Within three months of his death Roberto Clemente, who was born on August 18, 1934, was elected to the Hall of Fame.

● *Determined Roberto Clemente of the Pittsburgh Pirates goes for a ball against the ivy-covered fence at Chicago's Wrigley Field.*

CLEVELAND INDIANS. The crowd of 56,715 at Cleveland's Municipal Stadium was lured mainly by the presence of Frank Robinson, the first black ever to manage in the major leagues. Robinson's first move that cold April day of 1975 was to insert himself in the batting order as the designated hitter.

And Robinson the hitter made Robinson the manager look good when he blasted a home run in the first inning to send the Indians to a 5–3 victory over the Yankees.

It was not the first time the two teams were linked in history. Between the years 1947 and 1958 the Yankees won 10 pennants; the team that kept them from making it 12 straight was the Indians. In 1948 the Indians won a one-game playoff over the Boston Red Sox for the pennant, then polished off another Boston entry, the Braves, in the World Series. After chasing the Yanks without success for the next five years, the Indians had an unbelievable season in 1954, winning 111 games and the pennant. Pitchers Bob Lemon, Early Wynn, Mike Garcia, Art Houtteman, and Bob Feller combined to post 78 victories; Al Rosen, Larry Doby, and Bobby Avila were the hitting stars. It was the third and last pennant in Cleveland history.

In the franchise's early days the Indians had their share of great players, starting with Cy Young, who won 268 of his 511 victories for them. Then came Napoleon Lajoie, who was so outstanding that the team was called the Naps while he was on it. The legendary Tris Speaker joined the team in 1916 and managed it to its first pennant four years later.

● *A mainstay of the Indians for nearly 20 years, Bob Feller greets the press after pitching the second of his three no-hitters—this one against the Yankees in 1946.*

Feller, who hurled 3 no-hitters and 12 one-hitters in his brilliant 266-win career, was the backbone of the pitching staff for almost 20 years.

Besides Feller, Lemon, Speaker, Lajoie, Young, and Wynn, Cleveland can take pride in these other Indians who made the Hall of Fame: Jesse Burkett, Elmer Flick, Sam Rice, Stanley Coveleski, Satchel Paige, Earl Averill, Joe Sewell, Addie Joss, Lou Boudreau, a player-manager at the age of 24, and manager Al Lopez.

CLOWN. A player with a sense of humor or an entertainer who is part of a baseball sideshow before games, between games of a doubleheader, and so on. He is there to help amuse the fans.

The most famous baseball clown, Al Schacht, a pitcher with the Washington Senators in the 1920s of limited skill but great humor, became a successful New York restaurant owner. Schacht's antics at major- and minor-league ballparks brought him the title Clown Prince of Baseball.

Another successful baseball clown is Max Patkin, who works mainly in the minor leagues. Like Schacht, Patkin also is a former pitcher, but one who never made the major leagues.

● *San Diego's KGB Chicken became a favorite of the fans in the late 1970s and later took his act to ballparks around the nation.*

● *Max Patkin's antics always drew a crowd and a laugh.*

● *Al Schacht, the Clown Prince (left), worked with partner Nick Altrock.*

CLUTCH. A player who constantly comes through tough spots is known as a clutch-hitter or pitcher, or a money player. Such a player was Tommy Henrich of the New York Yankees. During the late 1940s Henrich was such a successful clutch-hitter that he was dubbed Old Reliable. Another was Hank Aaron of the Milwaukee (later Atlanta) Braves and the Milwaukee Brewers, called Money in the Bank or Mr. Chips by his teammates because he usually delivered in important situations. Among the all-time clutch-hitters are Tony Perez, Reggie Jackson, and Pete Rose.

COACH. One of the manager's assistants, almost always a former player. Coaches serve as hitting, pitching and fielding instructors. When a team is at bat, one coach is stationed near first base and one near third base to direct the base runners, if there are any.

COBB, TY. The runner arrived in a cloud of dust, spikes high, barreling into the bag as the fielder stepped gingerly out of the way. Credit Ty Cobb with another stolen base.

Cobb was the most successful base runner of his day and the very best hitter in the history of baseball. He stole 96 bases in one season and 892 over his career, and both records stood for decades as the measure of running ability. Cobb worked hard on the baseball diamond, playing the game with a vengeance and running the bases with daring.

It's obvious that you can't steal first base, and Cobb didn't have to. Three thousand hits is considered the measure of a first-quality hitter. Cobb, however, is the only player in the history of the game to get more than 4,000 hits. He finished his career with an awesome total of 4,191 hits in 24 seasons with the Detroit Tigers and Philadelphia Athletics. That's more than 500 more than

• *Slashing spikes and a remarkable bat made Ty Cobb (left) a legend on the diamond.*

any other player had managed through the 1981 season.

Cobb batted a remarkable .367 for his career and soared over .400 three times with a high point of .420 in 1911 when he had 248 hits in 591 at-bats. That was one of nine batting titles in a row. He won 12 batting championships overall.

Cobb, who was born on December 18, 1886, in Narrows, Georgia, received the most votes in the first Hall of Fame election in 1936. He died on July 17, 1961.

COLLAR. Going through an entire game without getting a hit. If a player fails to hit, he is said to have gotten the collar.

COMMISSIONER. Baseball's top-ranking administrator. One was appointed after disputes among major-league owners, capped by the revelation that several members of the Chicago White Sox conspired with gamblers to purposely lose the 1919 World Series to the Cincinnati Reds.

In an attempt to restore public confidence in the game, baseball appointed the respect-

ed Judge Kenesaw Mountain Landis as its first commissioner. He served from 1921 to his death in 1944, when he was succeeded by Albert B. (Happy) Chandler, former governor of Kentucky. Chandler reigned until 1950, when the owners voted him out of office and gave the job to National League president Ford C. Frick, who retired after the 1965 season.

As Frick's successor the baseball owners selected William D. Eckert, a retired lieutenant-general of the U.S. Air Force. Eckert took up his duties beginning with the 1966 season. In 1969 Eckert was fired, and Bowie K. Kuhn, former counsel to the National League, became baseball's fifth commissioner. An owners' revolt to oust Kuhn in 1975 failed and, instead, he was elected to a new seven-year term.

The commissioner's major duties include settling grievances of players, clubs, or leagues in organized baseball, including the minor leagues; investigating and punishing acts that he believes may hurt baseball; and running the World Series. In addition to the commissioner, each league has its own president—Lee MacPhail in the American League and Charles (Chub) Feeney in the National League are the current presidents —whose functions are to act in the manner of a commissioner within their leagues.

• *The first commissioner: Judge Kenesaw Mountain Landis*

CONTRACT. All major- and minor-league teams hire players on a contract basis. In the winter the clubs enjoy a great amount of publicity by announcing day after day that this player or that one has signed his contract, come to terms, inked his pact.

COUNT. The number of balls and strikes on a batter. The highest count is three and two—three balls and two strikes —which is known as a full count.

CURVE. One of the two standard pitches of baseball, the other being the fastball. The orthodox curveball is thrown with a decided snap and twist of the wrist. A right-hander's curve breaks from right to left as he faces the plate; a left-hander's curve breaks from left to right.

The sinker or drop is a curve that breaks down as well as out. Most curveballs sink, some more sharply than others. A slider is a fast curve with small break, sometimes called a nickel curve. It is probably the most widely used pitch, since it gets its effectiveness from breaking late, is easier to control, and causes less strain on the pitcher's arm. By the time it breaks, the hitter may be swinging in the wrong place or he may let it go only to see it slip into the strike zone. A curveball is also known as a jug (for jug handle), rainbow, dipsy-do, hook, and snake. Among the more talented curveball pitchers have been Sal Maglie, Johnny Sain, Camilo Pascual, Mike Flanagan, and Bert Blyleven.

The curveball was first used in 1867 by W.A. Cummings. There have been many claims by scientists that a curveball is nothing more than an optical illusion. To dispute such claims, pitcher Freddie Fitzsimmons of the Brooklyn Dodgers staged a demonstration that silenced the doubters for good. On December 1, 1941, he set up three posts in a straight line between himself and home plate, 60 feet and 6 inches away. He re-

● *Bert Blyleven readies his curve.*

leased the ball to the right of the first post and made it go to the left of the second post and to the right of the third post.

Whitlow Wyatt, also a Dodger pitcher of that time, offered to perform a more spectacular demonstration. Anyone who did not believe that a curveball curves could stand behind a tree, Wyatt proposed, "and I'll whomp him to death with an optical illusion." There were no takers.

CUTDOWN DATE. That time of year when a team must cut its roster to the maximum number of players allowed, by trading players, selling them, or sending them to the minor leagues. The maximum number of players a team is allowed is now 25, and the cutdown date is opening day.

CUTOFF. The interception of a thrown ball, usually from the 'outfield, for the purpose of trapping a runner off base or attempting to keep a runner or runners from advancing. If performed properly, it is one of the most exciting and important plays in the game. Its importance was obvious in the final game of the 1962 World Series.

The Yankees led the Giants, 1–0, with two out in the last of the ninth, a man on first, and Willie Mays at bat. Mays hit a line drive down the right-field line, a ball that would normally score a man from first. But Roger Maris raced over, picked up the ball on the run, and threw quickly to the cutoff, second baseman Bobby Richardson, who had gone into short right field for the throw. Richardson turned and threw quickly, strongly, and accurately to home plate, preventing the tying run from scoring. The next batter lined out, and the Yankees had won the game and the World Series, largely because Maris and Richardson had performed the cutoff play to perfection.

CYCLE. When a batter hits a single, double, triple, and home run, not necessarily in that order but all in the same game, it is called hitting for the cycle. It is so rare a feat that a couple of years may go by without it happening in the major leagues.

CY YOUNG AWARD. *See* Young, Cy.

DEAN, JAY AND PAUL. *See* Dizzy and Daffy.

DEATH VALLEY. The most spacious part of any ballpark, so called because to hit a ball there is almost certain death (a sure out). The best known Death Valley is left-center field in Yankee Stadium, which measures 430 feet from the plate. When the St. Louis Cardinals arrived at Yankee Stadium for the third game of the 1964 World Series, Lou Brock took one look at Death Valley and said, "There's a lot of room out there."

"That's no room," said Curt Flood, "that's a penthouse."

DEKED. Short for "decoy" or "decoyed," usually used by a batter who expects a fastball and gets a curve.

DESIGNATED HITTER. A rule adopted by the American League in 1973 which allows each team to appoint a hitter to substitute at bat for the pitcher. That hitter need not play in the field, but he may take a regular turn at bat in place of the pitcher, in any position in the batting order the manager chooses to insert him.

DEAD BALL. A ball legally out of play that results in a temporary suspension of play. Examples are a fair ball that hits a base runner, or a foul ball.

DETROIT TIGERS. One was a portly left-hander named Mickey Lolich who loved to ride a motorcycle. The other was a free-spirited right-hander named

● *Mark (The Bird) Fidrych provided comic relief—he's with Big Bird of Sesame Street—and won 19 games for the Detroit Tigers in 1976.*

Cobb led Detroit to three pennants in a row, from 1907 to 1909. The team didn't win another one until 1934, when the hitting of Charlie Gehringer and Hank Greenberg sparked the Tigers to the first of two straight flags. The team won the World Series in 1935, under player-manager Mickey Cochrane, and three years later the mighty Greenberg slammed 58 home runs. Greenberg was still on the team in 1945 when Detroit won its second world championship and southpaw Hal Newhouser was a 25-game winner.

Among the modern-era Tigers nobody could compare for popularity and performance with Kaline, but there have been others who caught the baseball world's fancy, like pitcher Mark (The Bird) Fidrych and outfielder Ron LeFlore, who learned to play baseball in prison.

DEUCE. Players' name for the curveball. The term is a carryover from sandlot days, when the catcher's signals to the pitcher were simply one finger for the fastball, two for the curve.

DIAMOND. Originally the infield, which is shaped like a diamond, but now expanded to include the entire field.

Denny McLain. They became the pitching story of 1968 when McLain won 31 games during the regular season and Lolich hurled three complete-game victories as the Tigers upset the St. Louis Cardinals in the World Series.

That marked the third world championship for a franchise that has featured some of the greatest hitters of all time. From Ty Cobb to Al Kaline to Norm Cash, the Tigers have boasted 22 American League batting champions, led by Ty Cobb, who won the title 12 times.

DIMAGGIO, JOE. The streak began innocently enough on May 15, 1941, with one hit in four at-bats, a single. Joe DiMaggio of the Yankees could never have known that at that moment he had begun a unique voyage through the baseball record book.

Day after day DiMaggio continued to punish pitchers with anywhere from one to four hits per game. On June 29 DiMaggio broke George Sisler's American League record of 41 straight games. Three days later, on July

• *The classic Joe DiMaggio swing produced a hitting streak of 56 games in 1941.*

2, Wee Willie Keeler's 44-game major-league record tumbled.

The end finally came on July 17 in Cleveland when two brilliant plays by Cleveland third baseman Ken Keltner stopped DiMaggio and, after 56 games, the hitting streak was over. It has never been broken.

Born on November 25, 1914, in Martinez, California, DiMaggio became an American folk hero. He played the outfield with style and grace and was one of the finest hitters of his time.

The Yankee Clipper won two batting championships and two MVP trophies. When he retired after the 1951 season, he had a career batting average of .325, with 361 home runs and a ticket to baseball's Hall of Fame.

DIZZY AND DAFFY. Nicknames of the famous Dean brothers of the 1930s, Jay Hanna (Dizzy) Dean and Paul Dee (Daffy) Dean, who came out of Arkansas with little education and captivated the public with their pranks on and off the field. Dizzy, the older, more successful, and zanier of the two, became a successful broadcaster and telecaster whose trademark was telling stories in his country jargon and singing country songs on the air.

Once the mother of a young boy scolded Dizzy for his horrible grammar on the air, which, she said, was a bad example for her son. "You don't even know the king's English," the woman said.

"Old Diz knows the king's English," Dean protested, "and not only that, I also know the queen is English."

Despite their reputation as characters, the Dean brothers were among the best pitchers of their day. Dizzy won 20 or more games in four straight years for the St. Louis Cardinals, was the last National League pitcher to win 30 games (30-7 in 1934), and achieved 150 victories before his career was shortened by a foot injury. Brother Paul twice

● *Dizzy (left) and Paul (Daffy) Dean were a colorful combo who pitched the St. Louis Cardinals to the world championship in 1934.*

won 19 games for the Cardinals. In 1934 the brothers won 49 games between them, pitching the Cardinals to the pennant, then won all 4 games as the Cardinals defeated the Detroit Tigers in the World Series.

DOUBLE. A two-base hit. Also called a two-bagger. Tris Speaker, whose career spanned 22 years and four American League teams, hit a record 793 doubles. Stan Musial of the St. Louis Cardinals holds the National League record of 725 lifetime doubles.

DOUBLEHEADER. Two games for the price of one. Also known as a bargain bill or twin bill. It has been a feature of the baseball schedule since 1882. The second game of a doubleheader has long been known as the nightcap or afterpiece. In recent years some teams introduced what is called the day-night doubleheader, which isn't a doubleheader at all. It is two games for the price of two games that just happen to be played on the same day.

● *Milwaukee's Robin Yount goes for the double play.*

DOUBLE PLAY. The act of getting two men out on a single play, in a continuous sequence. It is also known as a twin killing and, among players, as getting two. The Philadelphia Athletics made a record 217 double plays during the 1949 season, and the New York Yankees made a record seven double plays in one game on August 14, 1942. While it is desirable to make many double plays, it is not always a sign of strength, because for a team to make a record number of double plays, it must have an unusual number of opposition players on base during the season.

The most famous of all double-play combinations was the one known as Tinker-to-Evers-to-Chance. Joe Tinker, shortstop; Johnny Evers, second baseman; and Frank Chance, first baseman, played together for the Chicago Cubs from 1902 to 1912 and helped the Cubs win three straight pennants, in 1906, 1907, and 1908. Although this double-play combination was not the greatest of all time, it was the most feared of its day and inspired Franklin P. Adams of the New York *Evening Mail* to immortalize them with this poem:

These are the saddest of possible words:
    "Tinker to Evers to Chance."
Trio of bear Cubs and fleeter than birds,
    "Tinker to Evers to Chance."
Ruthlessly pricking our gonfalon bubble,
    Making a Giant hit into a double—
Words that are heavy with nothing but trouble:
    "Tinker to Evers to Chance."

DOUBLE STEAL. Two base runners successfully stealing bases on the same play.

DOWN THE ALLEY. A pitch thrown through the middle of the strike zone, frequently an automatic strike.

DRAFT. There are three. One is the free-agent draft, in which clubs get to choose—in reverse order of how they finished the season before—the eligible high-school and college players. The second permits a team to select players from other clubs' minor-league teams when those players have spent a certain number of years in the minors without a promotion to the majors. The third kind of draft is the free-agent re-entry draft, in which veteran major leaguers who choose to be free agents are selected, and often command big contracts.

DRAG BUNT. A bunt pulled down the first-base line by a left-handed hitter. A bunt in the same direction by a right-handed hitter is a push bunt. A bunt toward the third-base line by either type of batter is dropped or dumped, while "laying one down" is an expression that applies to bunting in general. A drag bunt is the favorite device of many fast runners because it is a virtual certainty that they will make first base safely if the bunt is well placed. Among the more effective drag bunters have been Mickey Mantle of the Yankees, Maury Wills of the Dodgers, and Rod Carew of the Twins and Angels.

DUGOUT. The area with a long bench for players, substitutes, and other team members not in the game. It gets its name from the fact it is dug into the ground so that part of the dugout is below the playing field.

DUST BOWL. A dusty field that has not been watered enough so that, at times, players feel like they are actors in the film *Lawrence of Arabia*.

DUSTER. A pitch thrown close to the batter's head, to keep the batter from taking a toehold at the plate. Unlike the beanball, a duster does not usually hit a batter, but accidents can happen, and some dusters become beanballs, intentionally or not. Also called a brushback pitch. When a player has been dusted or brushed back so that he has to fall to the ground to avoid being hit, he says he was decked or flipped. If he is hit, he has been beaned (in the head) or plugged (elsewhere).

● *Kansas City's George Brett is ducking from a duster thrown by Philadelphia's Dickie Noles in the 1980 World Series.*

EARNED RUN. A run for which the pitcher is held accountable, as opposed to an unearned run, which scores as the direct or indirect result of an error, passed ball, interference, or obstruction.

EARNED-RUN AVERAGE. A method of evaluating the efficiency of a pitcher, determined by dividing the total number of earned runs off his pitching by the total number of innings he has pitched, then multiplying by nine. This gives the pitcher's earned-run average, or ERA, for a nine-inning game—that is, the number of earned runs he has allowed for every nine innings. Anything under three earned runs per game is considered good. The lowest ERA on record for 300 innings or more is 1.12 by Bob Gibson of the St. Louis Cardinals in 1968.

EMERY BALL. A ball that has been illegally roughed up by rubbing a piece of sandpaper over its surface, causing it, when thrown, to rise, fall, or break away suddenly and unexpectedly. This was a common practice in the 1920s, but it was declared illegal.

ERROR. A fielding mistake charged for each fumble or wild throw that prolongs the time of a batter at bat, or the stay of a runner on base, or that permits a runner to advance or a batter to reach base safely. Kicking one or booting one is the players' usual parlance for making an error. Errors have become less frequent through the years as players' skills and their gloves improve.

EXHIBITION GAME. A baseball game that has no bearing on the official records of either the players or the teams, such as spring-training games and barnstorming games. Teams play a full schedule of 20 to 30 exhibition games in spring training in order to 1. help pay spring-training expenses by charging admission, 2. get advance publicity, and 3. enable the manager to evaluate the strengths and weaknesses of both his team and the opposition. An annual exhibition game is played each year at the Baseball Hall of Fame in Cooperstown, New York, as part of a ceremony during which members are inducted into the Hall of Fame. In recent years exhibition games have also been scheduled during the season, usually for the benefit of charity.

EXTRA-BASE HIT. A hit that is good for more than one base, for example, a two-base hit (double), three-base hit (triple), or four-base hit (home run). Also called long hits.

Babe Ruth holds the record for having made 119 extra-base hits in one season (44 doubles, 16 triples, and 59 home runs in 1921). Four players since 1900 have made five extra-base hits in one game: Joe Adcock of the Milwaukee Braves, who hit four home runs and one double on July 31, 1954; Lou Boudreau, who hit four doubles and one home run for Cleveland on July 14, 1946; Willie Stargell, who hit two home runs and three doubles for Pittsburgh on August 1, 1970; and Steve Garvey, who did the same for Los Angeles on August 28, 1977.

EXTRA INNINGS. When a game is tied after nine innings, play continues until one team has scored more runs than the other in a completed inning, or until the team batting last takes the lead. On May 1, 1920, the Boston Braves and the Brooklyn Dodgers struggled through a 1–1, 26-inning game, the longest ever played in the major leagues. Both starting pitchers, Joe Oeschger and Leon Cadore, lasted the whole game.

On May 31, 1964, the New York Mets and the San Francisco Giants played 23 innings, the Giants winning, 8–6, in the second game of a doubleheader. It was the longest game, in terms of time, ever played in the major leagues, ending at 11:18 p.m., exactly 7 hours and 32 minutes after it started.

The longest night game started at Shea Stadium, New York, on September 11, 1974, and ended 25 innings (7 hours and 4 minutes) later, the following morning. St. Louis beat the Mets, 4–3.

The longest scoreless game in history took place between the Astros and the Mets on April 16, 1968, at the Astrodome. The Astros won on an unearned run in the twenty-fourth inning.

FAIR BALL. A legally batted ball that is hit within the foul lines.

FAN. To strike out swinging; to fan the breeze. The term also means a rooter or a supporter of a team or of baseball in general, and is a short form of the word "fanatic."

• *The scoreboard at New York's Shea Stadium says it for a game that went 24 innings.*

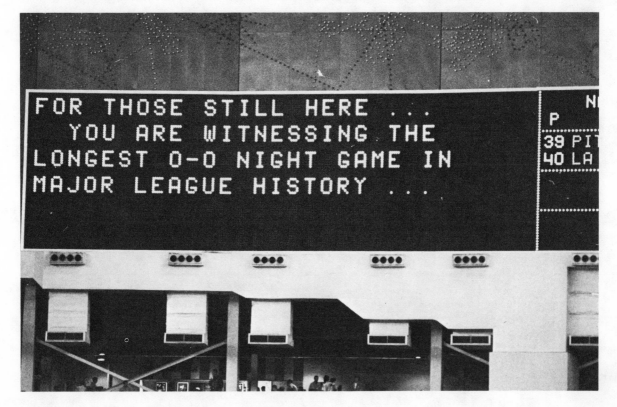

FARM SYSTEM. Branch Rickey introduced chainstore baseball when he was running the St. Louis Cardinals in the 1920s. Big-league players had been optioned to the minors as far back as 1887, but Rickey was the first to build a network of farm teams controlled by the parent club through either ownership or exclusive agreements. Other teams borrowed the idea after it began producing pennants for the Cardinals.

There is, of course, more to a farm system than acquiring teams. The secret of success is to keep the farms (or minor leagues) stocked with good players and to know which players to advance and which to sell, and when.

FASTBALL. Also fireball, high hard one. The speediest pitch that a pitcher can throw. The most frequently used pitch in the game.

● *The camera catches a Bob Feller fastball.*

FELLER, BOB. When he was just 17 years old, Bob Feller started his first game as a major-league pitcher. He struck out 15 batters that day for the Cleveland Indians and began a career that would see him pitch three no-hitters and win 266 games, all with the Indians, from 1936 to 1956.

He was known as Rapid Robert, and he began throwing his fastball against the side of a barn on the family farm in Van Meter, Iowa, where he was born on November 3, 1918. In 1946 he struck out 348 batters, a major-league record that stood for 20 years until it was broken by Sandy Koufax.

He was elected to the Hall of Fame in 1962.

FENCE. Outfield fences have two major effects on the game. Their height and distance from the plate help control the number of home runs, and they also affect fielding, since outfielders must learn how far and at what angle a ball is likely to bounce off a given fence. Most major-league parks were built before distance hitting, or fence busting, came into fashion, and for many years the fences were beyond the range of the hitters. To keep up with the home-run craze, stands have been built in order to shorten the outfields of some parks, while inner fences have been strung across the outfields of others. The following table shows distances to the left-, center- (farthest point), and right-field fences in each park:

Distances of Outfield Fences (in feet)

AMERICAN LEAGUE				NATIONAL LEAGUE			
Ballpark	Left	Center	Right	Ballpark	Left	Center	Right
Baltimore	309	410	309	Atlanta	330	400	330
Boston	315	420	302	Chicago	355	400	353
California	333	404	333	Cincinnati	330	404	330
Chicago	352	445	352	Houston	340	406	340
Cleveland	320	400	320	Los Angeles	330	395	330
Detroit	340	440	325	Montreal	340	420	340
Kansas City	330	410	330	New York	341	410	341
Milwaukee	320	402	362	Philadelphia	330	408	330
Minnesota	330	430	373	Pittsburgh	335	400	335
New York	313	419	310	St. Louis	330	404	330
Oakland	330	400	330	San Diego	330	410	330
Seattle	316	410	316	San Francisco	335	410	335
Texas	330	400	330				
Toronto	330	400	300				

FIELD. To handle a batted or thrown ball while on the defense. Also, the area on which opponents do battle.

FIELDER'S CHOICE. The act of a fielder who catches a groundball and throws it to some base other than first, attempting to retire a runner already on base rather than the batter. There is the assumption that the fielder could have retired the batter, but chose to make a play on the preceding runner. Whether or not the fielder completes the play successfully, the batter is scored as having hit into a fielder's choice and is charged with an official time at bat and no hit.

FINE. A fee charged to a player by his manager, owner, league president, or the commissioner for any action believed harmful to his team, league, or all of baseball, or for breaking any rule set down by his team, league, or the baseball commissioner's office. In 1925 the largest fine up to that point ever levied on a player was slapped on Babe Ruth. His manager, Miller Huggins, had had his fill of the Babe's consistent violation of training regulations, so he fined Ruth $5,000.

There is a story that when Joe McCarthy followed Huggins as Yankee manager, he got Babe's $5,000 back, in an effort to win the big guy over. Babe also suffered the second largest fine, this one from Commissioner Landis in 1921. The Babe hit 59 home runs that year, and after the season he lined up an exhibition tour, which was against league rules. When Landis found out about it, he fined Babe his entire check from the 1921 World Series ($3,362.26) and suspended him until May 20, 1922, so that Ruth also lost a month's pay.

In 1965 pitcher Juan Marichal of the San Francisco Giants hit John Roseboro, catcher for the Los Angeles Dodgers, on the head with a baseball bat. Marichal was suspended nine days in the midst of a close pennant race and was fined $1,750.

In 1980 Bill Madlock, third baseman for the Pittsburgh Pirates, was hit with the largest fine in National League history when he slapped umpire Jerry Crawford across the face with his glove. He had to pay $5,000 and was suspended for 15 days.

FIRST BALL. A pregame ceremony usually associated with opening day of the season and the President of the United States. It all began in 1910 when President William Howard Taft attended the season's starter between the Washington Senators and the Philadelphia Athletics. As an added touch Taft tossed out the first ball from his

● *President William Howard Taft threw out the first ball in 1910.*

box seat and began what has become a ritual practiced by most Presidents since then. Over the years the first-ball happening has preceded other important games, such as the playoffs and the World Series, and assorted dignitaries are usually chosen for the tossing.

FIRST BASE. The base to which the batter runs first, a 15-inch-square bag located diagonally to the right and 90 feet from home plate. The defensive player whose duty it is to cover the area around first base is the first baseman.

FLY BALL. A batted ball that goes high in the air.

FLY-OUT. A fairly hit ball that is caught before it touches the ground by a fielder—usually, but not always, an outfielder.

FOOT IN THE BUCKET. A batting stance in which the front foot is withdrawn toward the foul line (toward the old water bucket in the dugout) instead of pointing toward the pitcher. Often such a stance is a sign of timidity, the foot being planted that way to give the batter a head start in getting out of the way of a close pitch. But the foot-in-the-bucket stance has been used by a number of outstanding hitters, among them Al Simmons, who had a lifetime batting average of .334 for 20 big-league seasons; Roy Campanella; and Arky Vaughan.

FORCED OUT. A fielder retiring a base runner by touching the base to which the runner is forced to advance. The only time a force play happens is when there is a runner on first base, runners on first and second, or runners on first, second, and third, and a batted ball hits the ground, either in the infield or the outfield. In each case the runner already on base is forced out if he doesn't reach the next base ahead of the ball.

FORFEIT. Any one of several rules violations, most of them concerned with the refusal of a team or player to continue playing, may cause the umpire to declare the game forfeited. The forfeit score is 9–0 in favor of the offended team.

FORKBALL. A ball that is pitched by being held at the top with the index and middle fingers wide apart (like a fork) and at the bottom by the thumb. In its delivery it breaks like the knuckleball. The leading user of the forkball was Elroy Face, who pitched it to win 18 games and lose only one for the Pittsburgh Pirates in 1959.

FOUL BALL. Any legally batted ball that lands in foul territory, whether it is a fly ball or a groundball, a ball tipped by the batter or one hit out of the park. A foul ball is a strike unless it is caught on the fly by a fielder, in which case the batter is out. If a ball is tipped by the batter, it is a strike; if there are already two strikes on the batter, the batter is out, and the pitcher is credited with a strikeout. A foul ball is not an automatic third strike if the batter already has two strikes on him. However, if the batter has two strikes and he tries to bunt, and it goes foul, he is automatically out.

FOXX, JIMMIE. He was a barrel-chested son of a farmer and he slugged home runs with the strength of a mule. Jimmie Foxx was known as Double X, and from 1925 to 1945 he drove 534 homers, most of them for the Philadelphia A's and the Boston Red Sox.

Foxx, born on October 22, 1907, in Sudlersville, Maryland, hit 58 homers in 1932, was voted the American League's Most Valuable Player three times, and ended with a .325 lifetime batting average.

His biggest year came in 1933 when he won the Triple Crown—48 homers, 169 runs batted in, a .364 batting average—the league leader in all three categories.

Double X, chiefly a first baseman, also caught, played third and the outfield, and even pitched in 10 games. He was elected to the Hall of Fame in 1951 and died in 1967.

FRANCHISE. The right granted by a governing body to run a business in a certain place. In baseball it is the right granted by the commissioner for a person or persons to operate a team in a particular city.

FREE AGENT. Any player who is not under contract to a team and is, therefore, free to sign a contract. He may be a young player who has never been under contract or an older one who has gotten a release from his contract, such as Catfish Hunter, who was declared a free agent by a judge in 1974 because his Oakland contract had been breached. He then signed with the New York Yankees for $2.8 million for five years.

By 1980 salaries had increased at an incredible rate and several free agents owned million-dollar-a-year contracts. This was all part of the background for the 1981 baseball players' strike. (*See also* Draft; Major League Baseball Players Association.)

FUNGO. A ball hit to the infield or outfield during fielding practice. Fungoes are hit with a specially constructed thin, light bat, called a fungo stick. The fungo hitter tosses the ball a few feet in the air and swings, directing fly balls at the outfielders or groundballs at the infielders. The practice is run by a coach, who usually takes pride in his precision with a fungo stick. A dying art, however, is the trick of fungoing a high pop-up straight overhead for the catcher. The word "fungible" means one thing that

● *The day free agent Dave Winfield got his Yankee pinstripes.*

can be substituted for another, and it is thought that in baseball the thin fungo stick got its name because it replaces the conventional bat.

GAME. A game of baseball consists of 9 full innings, each team having 9 turns at bat, except when the home team is ahead after 8½ innings, at which point the game ends automatically. A game is also considered finished if play is halted (by rain, snow, and so on) after the team that is trailing has been to bat at least five times.

GASHOUSE GANG. A nickname given to the St. Louis Cardinals of the 1930s because they were a collection of rowdy, fiery, daring players who included manager Frank Frisch, Pepper Martin, Ducky Medwick, Leo Durocher, and Dizzy Dean. Frank Graham, then with the New York *Sun,* suggested to Durocher that the Cardinals were so good that they could win in any league, including the powerful American League. "They wouldn't let us play in the American League," Durocher corrected. "They'd say we were just a lot of gashouse players." Graham picked up the expression, started calling the Cardinals the Gashouse Gang, and the name stuck.

GEHRIG, LOU. On June 2, 1925, New York Yankee first baseman Wally Pipp asked for the day off, complaining of a headache. Manager Miller Huggins chose a rookie, 22-year-old Lou Gehrig, to take Pipp's place, and for the next 2,130 games

● *It was a tearful time for all when illness forced Lou Gehrig's retirement in 1939.*

Gehrig was never out of the Yankee lineup.

Born in New York on June 19, 1903, the Iron Horse played most of his career in the shadow of the more colorful Babe Ruth, but he was a mighty hitter in his own right. He played briefly at Columbia University before launching a professional career that would see him lead the league in homers three times (sharing it once with Ruth), drive in 150 or more runs seven times, hit four home runs in one game, and set a major-league record that still stands for most home runs with the bases full: 23.

Larrupin' Lou was the American League's Most Valuable Player in 1927 and 1936, belted 493 home runs, and had a lifetime batting average of .340.

He didn't leave the Yankee lineup until May 2, 1939, when a crippling illness—poliomyelitis—forced his retirement. He died in 1941, two years after he was voted into the Hall of Fame.

63 ●

• *Bob Gibson was supreme in the World Series.*

GIBSON, BOB.

The pitching match-up was perfect for a World Series setting. For Detroit, 31-game-winner Denny McLain, the first pitcher since 1931 to win more than 30. For St. Louis, Bob Gibson, enjoying a dream year that included a 1.12 earned-run average, the lowest in history for a 300-inning season.

This was the opening game of the 1968 World Series between the Tigers and the Cardinals, each with a powerhouse pitcher. But it was no match. McLain was gone by the sixth inning. Gibson, meanwhile, mowed down the Tigers, setting a Series record with 17 strikeouts on the way to a 4–0 victory.

Gibson was at his absolute best in World Series competition. He won seventh-game Series assignments in 1964 and 1967. In 9 World Series starts, he finished 8 games, compiled a 7-2 record with a 1.89 ERA, and recorded 92 strikeouts in 81 innings.

Gibby was a very basic pitcher, armed with an explosive fastball that challenged hitters. More often than not, he won that challenge.

Born on November 19, 1935, in Omaha, Nebraska, Gibson was a four-sport star at Creighton University and played for the Harlem Globetrotters for one year before turning to baseball. He pitched 16 full seasons for the Cardinals, finishing with 251 career victories and 3,117 strikeouts, third on the all-time list. Those accomplishments earned his election to the Hall of Fame in 1981.

GLOVE.

Originally intended for protection of the hand, the glove became a fielding aid as well. The early gloves were form-fitting. As late as 1920 George Sisler's first-baseman's mitt was scarcely larger than his hand. Today's gloves, particularly first-basemen's trapper models, are enormous, wide-webbed affairs that have led to a general improvement in fielding.

GLOVE MAN.

An outstanding fielder, also called a leather man. Among the best glove men is Mark Belanger of the Baltimore Orioles. The term is usually, but not necessarily, applied to infielders. Brooks Robinson of the Orioles, Billy Cox of the Brooklyn Dodgers, and Marty Marion of the St. Louis Cardinals were great glove men.

• *Baltimore's Brooks Robinson shows what makes a glove man in the 1970 World Series against Cincinnati.*

GOPHER. A pitch hit for a home run. First used when Lefty Gomez pitched for the Yankees. Writers joked about his gopher ball, which would "go fer the stands" or "go fer four bases." The all-time gopher champion is Robin Roberts, who threw 46 gopher balls when he was with the Philadelphia Phillies in 1956. Ironically, Roberts still won 19 games that year.

GRAND SLAM. Home run with the bases full, sometimes called a jackpot. Lou Gehrig hit 23 career grand slams, the major-league record. Willie McCovey holds the National League record, with 18 for the San Francisco Giants and San Diego Padres. Ernie Banks of the Chicago Cubs set the record for grand slams in a season, with five in 1955, and it was tied by Jim Gentile in 1961 when he was with the Baltimore Orioles. In that year Gentile also tied Tony Lazzeri of the New York Yankees, Jim Tabor of the Boston Red Sox, and Rudy York of the Red Sox by hitting two grand slams in one game. Since then Jim Northrup, Frank Robinson, and Tony Cloninger have done the same.

● *Willie McCovey's 18 grand slams are a National League record.*

GRANDSTAND PLAY. A comparatively easy fielding play made to look more difficult by a player who wants to attract the spectators' attention.

GRAPEFRUIT LEAGUE. General term for spring training, technically referring to exhibition games played in Florida and differing from the Cactus League in Arizona. In theory, the idea of spring training is to get the athletes into playing condition, aided by a warm climate, but it has equal if not greater value as an extended publicity stunt that keeps baseball in the headlines for two months before the season opens. Even southern minor-league teams pitch camp away from home on the theory that distance lends magic to their doings.

The Chicago White Stockings started the custom when they trained in New Orleans in 1870. By the 1890s the practice had become general, although the teams were still treated like outcasts. Connie Mack, remembering a trip to Jacksonville, Florida, with the Washington Senators in 1888, said, "The hotel clerk made the strict stipulation that the ballplayers would not mingle with the other guests or eat in the same dining room."

Eventually the clubs were welcomed as a tourist attraction. Thanks to a Florida booster named Al Lang, who first invited teams to his area in 1914, the Tampa Bay region has long been the center of big-league training activity. As a tribute to Al Lang, the field in St. Petersburg on which the St. Louis Cardinals and New York Mets play their spring-training games is called Al Lang Field.

GROUNDER. Also groundball, roller, bouncer, hopper, grass cutter. A batted ball that rolls or bounces on the ground to an infielder or through the infield for a hit.

GROUND OUT. To hit a groundball to an infielder and be thrown out at first base.

GROUND RULES. Special rules covering conditions in a given park. Most ground rules have to do with whether or not a batted ball or thrown ball is in play if it strikes certain obstacles on the sidelines or on the walls.

A funny incident concerning ground rules happened during the 1965 World Series. A guest at the first game was Vice President Hubert Humphrey, who sat next to the Minnesota Twins' dugout on the first-base side. It became part of the ground rules for the game that any ball was still in play if it hit the Secret Service man sitting on the field guarding the vice president.

HALF SWING. The action of a batter trying to stop his swing, but failing to do so. Even a half swing counts as a whole strike.

HALL OF FAME. Baseball maintains a Hall of Fame honoring outstanding players, managers, umpires, and others connected with the game. Proposed by Ford Frick in 1935 soon after he became National League president, it was begun the next year with the election of Ty Cobb, Walter Johnson, Christy Mathewson, Babe Ruth, and Honus Wagner. There are now more than 150 members.

The method of selection has varied from time to time, but under present regulations, members are chosen each year from two categories by two independent groups. To qualify for the Hall of Fame, a player must have been retired at least five years. Members of the Baseball Writers' Association of America vote on players who have been out of the game for at least 5 but not more than

GEORGE HERMAN (BABE) RUTH
BOSTON—NEW YORK, A.L.; BOSTON, N.L.
1915 – 1935
GREATEST DRAWING CARD IN HISTORY OF BASEBALL. HOLDER OF MANY HOME RUN AND OTHER BATTING RECORDS. GATHERED 714 HOME RUNS IN ADDITION TO FIFTEEN IN WORLD SERIES.

• *Babe Ruth's plaque hangs with the other immortals' in the Baseball Hall of Fame in Cooperstown, New York.*

20 years. The Committee on Baseball Veterans (mostly writers and ex-baseball officials) votes on players of the more distant past and others who have distinguished themselves in various branches of the game, such as umpires, managers, sportswriters, and league and team officials.

Each year a baseball game between two major-league teams is played when new members are entered into the Hall of Fame. The actual Hall of Fame, containing bronze statues of those elected, is a room in the Baseball Museum in Cooperstown, New York, a site chosen in the now disputed belief that baseball was invented there by Abner Doubleday. Ironically, Doubleday is not in the Hall of Fame.

In addition to the bronze statues of the members, there are other mementos in the Hall of Fame that help make it a favorite tourist attraction. Among them are the bench Connie Mack sat on in the Philadelphia Athletic dugout for many years; a ball used in 1866; Stan Musial's spikes; the baseball with which Cy Young won his five-hundredth game; the lockers of Honus Wagner, Babe Ruth, Lou Gehrig, and Joe DiMaggio; and the sliding pads used by Ty Cobb when he stole 96 bases in 1915.

Besides the players, managers, and umpires elected to the Hall of Fame, others honored include Morgan Bulkeley, first president of the National League; Henry Chadwick, an early baseball writer credited with inventing the box score; commission-ers Kenesaw Mountain Landis, Ford Frick, and Alexander Cartwright, whom many historians recognize as the true founder of baseball rather than Doubleday.

HIT.   A hit, safety, safe blow, bingle, or base knock is a batted ball on which the batter reaches base without benefit of an error, fielder's choice, interference, or the retirement of a preceding runner. A one-

● *Nobody produced more hits than Ty Cobb, whose 4,191 safeties are not likely to be surpassed.*

base hit is a single, a two-base hit a double, a three-base hit a triple, and a four-base hit a home run.

The official scorer decides whether or not a hit has been made. Most hits are obvious and some are automatic, such as when a batted ball strikes an umpire or runner before touching a fielder, but there are close decisions in almost every game.

To the casual fan many a hit looks like an error. But the scorer must allow for such things as freak hops or drives that are smashed too hard for the fielder to handle smoothly. Often, when a slow groundball is fumbled, it will still be scored as a hit. Usually this brings a hoot from the stands, but the scorer may well have been right in deciding that the batter would have beaten it out even if the ball had been fielded cleanly.

Ty Cobb is baseball's all-time hit producer, having smacked out 4,191 in his 24-year major-league career. George Sisler made the most hits in one season, 257 for the St. Louis Browns in 1920—three more than Lefty O'Doul made for the Philadelphia Phillies in 1929 and Bill Terry for the New York Giants a year later. O'Doul and Terry share the National League record.

Many players have had six hits in one game, but Rennie Stennett of Pittsburgh made seven hits in a 9-inning game in 1975, and John Burnett of the Cleveland Indians made nine hits in an 18-inning game in 1932.

The standard of excellence is 200 hits in a season, and Pete Rose did it 10 times, a record. He is one of only 15 to make more than 3,000 hits in a career.

The team record for hits in a season is 1,783 by the Philadelphia Phillies in 1930. The New York Giants made 31 hits in a game in 1901, and the Boston Red Sox made 14 hits in one inning in 1953.

HIT-AND-RUN. A prearranged play in which the runner on first starts for sec- ond as the ball is pitched and the batter swings. Ideally, the batter pokes a hit through the spot left empty by the infielder who is drawn away to cover the base runner. This is a rare happening and used to be practiced with particular success by Maury Wills and Jim Gilliam of the Los Angeles Dodgers, but the hit-and-run can still be an effective weapon in avoiding double plays even if the batter does not achieve the desired result. The run-and-hit differs slightly from the hit-and-run in that the batter is not committed to hit the ball in the run-and-hit unless the pitch is to his liking.

HIT BATTER OR HIT BY PITCH. A batter hit by a pitched ball is entitled to first base, a rule that goes back to 1884, when a Cincinnati pitcher named Will White made a fetish of hitting batters in order to keep them at a respectable distance from the plate.

HITCH. A flaw in a batter's swing, considered undesirable because it goes against the theory that a batter must have a smooth swing to be effective. Many hitters have been successful even with a hitch.

HOLDOUT. A player who delays sign- ing his contract to bargain for more money. The most celebrated baseball holdout was Edd Roush, the old Cincinnati Red and New York Giant outfielder. In 1929 Roush hit .324 for the Giants in the last year of a three-year contract calling for $21,500 a year. Roush expected a raise, but when the Giants sent him his 1930 contract, it called for a cut. Roush and the Giants entered into a bitter dispute, with neither backing down. As a result Roush sat out the entire 1930 season.

In 1919 Zach Wheat, a Brooklyn Dodger outfielder, was unhappy with his contract. A war of nerves resulted between Wheat and Dodger owner Charley Ebbets. It was settled when Abe Yaeger, sports editor of the Brooklyn *Eagle,* sent the following wire to Wheat from the Dodgers' spring-training headquarters: "Report immediately." It was signed "Charley Ebbets." When Wheat reported, he had a good laugh with Ebbets over the joke. He then signed his contract.

Babe Ruth frequently held out. He once insisted on a raise over his previous year's salary of $50,000. Colonel Jake Ruppert, the Yankee owner, thought $50,000 was plenty. The Babe settled for $50,001.

Thanks to Babe's insistence on value for value, ballplayers' salaries in general were raised. In 1965 Willie Mays of the San Francisco Giants signed for the then highest salary of all time, $105,000, joining Joe DiMaggio, Stan Musial, Ted Williams, and Mickey Mantle in the $100,000 bracket. Since then salaries have soared to the extent that some players are earning more than a million dollars a year.

HOME RUN. A four-base hit also known as a homer; round-tripper; four-bagger; four-ply swat, blow, or wallop; circuit blow; four-master; or circuit clout. It is usually a ball driven out of the playing field, but a ball hit within the park that allows the batter to circle the bases also counts as a home run. When a batter hits one out of the park, it's an automatic home run but he must touch all the bases on the way back to home plate. If nobody is on base, it counts for one run. If one man is on base, it counts for two runs. And so on.

Babe Ruth set the big-league standard of 60 home runs in one season (1927) and 714 for a career, records that lasted for years and were believed unbreakable.

But in 1961 Roger Maris of the New York Yankees hit 61 home runs and set up a storm of controversy. First it was said that Maris hit his home runs during the era of

● *Babe Ruth hit 60 home runs in a season and 714 in his career.*

the lively ball (when the ball was thought to be made of different materials that would make it travel farther). Second, it was pointed out that he hit his home runs during a 162-game schedule, while Ruth hit his during a 154-game schedule (Maris had 59 home runs after 154 games). Commissioner Ford Frick decreed that Maris' record would stand, but with an asterisk noting the 162-game schedule, and that there would be *two* records—Ruth's for 154 games and Maris' for 162 games.

Ruth's career mark of 714 home runs lasted until April 8, 1974, when Hank Aaron hit number 715 for the Atlanta Braves against Al Downing and the Los Angeles Dodgers. Again, defenders of Ruth as the game's greatest slugger came forward to point out that Babe's 714 home runs came in 8,399 at-bats, while Aaron had been to bat over 11,000 times.

Ballplayers have other expressions for a home run. They say a batter "hit one downtown" or "went for the pump." Casey Stengel said that a batter "hit one over a building."

Sportscasters, too, have chipped in with their own expressions for baseball's most satisfying play. Many broadcasters use their home-run call as a trademark. Russ Hodges, who did the games for the San Francisco Giants, greeted each blast with "It's bye bye, baby." Others use "It's gone" or "It's out of here."

Whatever they use, you know when it's a home run, a homer, a circuit smash, or a four-ply swat.

● *Roger Maris' 61 homers produced a controversy.*

Home-Run Leaders

NATIONAL LEAGUE

Year	Player, Club	HR's	Year	Player, Club	HR's
1900	Herman Long, Boston Beaneaters	12	1939	Johnny Mize, St. Louis Cardinals	28
1901	Sam Crawford, Cincinnati Reds	16	1940	Johnny Mize, St. Louis Cardinals	43
1902	Tom Leach, Pittsburgh Pirates	6	1941	Dolph Camilli, Brooklyn Dodgers	34
1903	Jim Sheckard, Brooklyn Dodgers	9	1942	Mel Ott, New York Giants	30
1904	Harry Lumley, Brooklyn Dodgers	9	1943	Bill Nicholson, Chicago Cubs	29
1905	Fred Odwell, Cincinnati Reds	9	1944	Bill Nicholson, Chicago Cubs	33
1906	Tim Jordan, Brooklyn Dodgers	12	1945	Tommy Holmes, Boston Braves	28
1907	Dave Brain, Boston Doves	10	1946	Ralph Kiner, Pittsburgh Pirates	23
1908	Tim Jordan, Brooklyn Dodgers	12	1947	Ralph Kiner, Pittsburgh Pirates	51
1909	Jim Murray, New York Giants	7		Johnny Mize, New York Giants	51
1910	Fred Beck, Boston Doves	10	1948	Ralph Kiner, Pittsburgh Pirates	40
	Frank Schulte, Chicago Cubs	10		Johnny Mize, New York Giants	40
1911	Frank Schulte, Chicago Cubs	21	1949	Ralph Kiner, Pittsburgh Pirates	54
1912	Heinie Zimmerman, Chicago Cubs	14	1950	Ralph Kiner, Pittsburgh Pirates	47
1913	Gavvy Cravath, Philadelphia Phillies	19	1951	Ralph Kiner, Pittsburgh Pirates	42
1914	Gavvy Cravath, Philadelphia Phillies	19	1952	Ralph Kiner, Pittsburgh Pirates	37
1915	Gavvy Cravath, Philadelphia Phillies	24		Hank Sauer, Chicago Cubs	37
1916	Dave Robertson, New York Giants	12	1953	Eddie Mathews, Milwaukee Braves	47
	Cy Williams, Chicago Cubs	12	1954	Ted Kluszewski, Cincinnati Reds	49
1917	Gavvy Cravath, Philadelphia Phillies	12	1955	Willie Mays, New York Giants	51
	Dave Robertson, New York Giants	12	1956	Duke Snider, Brooklyn Dodgers	43
1918	Gavvy Cravath, Philadelphia Phillies	8	1957	Hank Aaron, Milwaukee Braves	44
1919	Gavvy Cravath, Philadelphia Phillies	12	1958	Ernie Banks, Chicago Cubs	47
1920	Cy Williams, Philadelphia Phillies	15	1959	Eddie Mathews, Milwaukee Braves	46
1921	George Kelly, New York Giants	23	1960	Ernie Banks, Chicago Cubs	41
1922	Rogers Hornsby, St. Louis Cardinals	39	1961	Orlando Cepeda, San Francisco Giants	46
1923	Cy Williams, Philadelphia Phillies	41	1962	Willie Mays, San Francisco Giants	49
1924	Jack Fournier, Brooklyn Dodgers	27	1963	Hank Aaron, Milwaukee Braves	44
1925	Rogers Hornsby, St. Louis Cardinals	39		Willie McCovey, San Francisco Giants	44
1926	Hack Wilson, Chicago Cubs	21	1964	Willie Mays, San Francisco Giants	47
1927	Cy Williams, Philadelphia Phillies	30	1965	Willie Mays, San Francisco Giants	52
	Hack Wilson, Chicago Cubs	30	1966	Hank Aaron, Atlanta Braves	44
1928	Jim Bottomley, St. Louis Cardinals	31	1967	Hank Aaron, Atlanta Braves	39
	Hack Wilson, Chicago Cubs	31	1968	Willie McCovey, San Francisco Giants	36
1929	Chuck Klein, Philadelphia Phillies	43	1969	Willie McCovey, San Francisco Giants	45
1930	Hack Wilson, Chicago Cubs	56	1970	Johnny Bench, Cincinnati Reds	45
1931	Chuck Klein, Philadelphia Phillies	31	1971	Willie Stargell, Pittsburgh Pirates	48
1932	Chuck Klein, Philadelphia Phillies	38	1972	Johnny Bench, Cincinnati Reds	40
	Mel Ott, New York Giants	38	1973	Willie Stargell, Pittsburgh Pirates	44
1933	Chuck Klein, Philadelphia Phillies	43	1974	Mike Schmidt, Philadelphia Phillies	36
1934	Rip Collins, St. Louis Cardinals	35	1975	Mike Schmidt, Philadelphia Phillies	38
	Mel Ott, New York Giants	35	1976	Mike Schmidt, Philadelphia Phillies	38
1935	Wally Berger, Boston Braves	34	1977	George Foster, Cincinnati Reds	52
1936	Mel Ott, New York Giants	33	1978	George Foster, Cincinnati Reds	40
1937	Joe Medwick, St. Louis Cardinals	31	1979	Dave Kingman, Chicago Cubs	48
	Mel Ott, New York Giants	31	1980	Mike Schmidt, Philadelphia Phillies	48
1938	Mel Ott, New York Giants	36	1981	Mike Schmidt, Philadelphia Phillies	31

Home-Run Leaders

AMERICAN LEAGUE

Year	Player, Club	HR's	Year	Player, Club	HR's
1901	Napoleon Lajoie, Philadelphia Athletics	13	1943	Rudy York, Detroit Tigers	34
1902	Ralph Seybold, Philadelphia Athletics	16	1944	Nick Etten, New York Yankees	22
1903	John Freeman, Boston Red Sox	13	1945	Vern Stephens, St. Louis Browns	24
1904	Harry Davis, Philadelphia Athletics	10	1946	Hank Greenberg, Detroit Tigers	44
1905	Harry Davis, Philadelphia Athletics	8	1947	Ted Williams, Boston Red Sox	32
1906	Harry Davis, Philadelphia Athletics	12	1948	Joe DiMaggio, New York Yankees	39
1907	Harry Davis, Philadelphia Athletics	8	1949	Ted Williams, Boston Red Sox	43
1908	Sam Crawford, Detroit Tigers	7	1950	Al Rosen, Cleveland Indians	37
1909	Ty Cobb, Detroit Tigers	9	1951	Gus Zernial, Philadelphia Athletics	33
1910	Garland Stahl, Boston Red Sox	10	1952	Larry Doby, Cleveland Indians	32
1911	Home Run Baker, Philadelphia Athletics	9	1953	Al Rosen, Cleveland Indians	43
1912	Home Run Baker, Philadelphia Athletics	10	1954	Larry Doby, Cleveland Indians	32
1913	Home Run Baker, Philadelphia Athletics	12	1955	Mickey Mantle, New York Yankees	37
1914	Home Run Baker, Philadelphia Athletics	8	1956	Mickey Mantle, New York Yankees	52
	Sam Crawford, Detroit Tigers	8	1957	Roy Sievers, Washington Senators	42
1915	Bob Roth, Cleveland Indians	7	1958	Mickey Mantle, New York Yankees	42
1916	Wally Pipp, New York Yankees	12	1959	Rocky Colavito, Cleveland Indians	42
1917	Wally Pipp, New York Yankees	9		Harmon Killebrew, Washington Senators	42
1918	Babe Ruth, Boston Red Sox	11	1960	Mickey Mantle, New York Yankees	40
	Clarence Walker, Philadelphia Athletics	11	1961	Roger Maris, New York Yankees	61
1919	Babe Ruth, Boston Red Sox	29	1962	Harmon Killebrew, Minnesota Twins	48
1920	Babe Ruth, New York Yankees	54	1963	Harmon Killebrew, Minnesota Twins	45
1921	Babe Ruth, New York Yankees	59	1964	Harmon Killebrew, Minnesota Twins	49
1922	Ken Williams, St. Louis Browns	39	1965	Tony Conigliaro, Boston Red Sox	32
1923	Babe Ruth, New York Yankees	43	1966	Frank Robinson, Baltimore Orioles	49
1924	Babe Ruth, New York Yankees	46	1967	Carl Yastrzemski, Boston Red Sox	44
1925	Bob Meusel, New York Yankees	33		Harmon Killebrew, Minnesota Twins	44
1926	Babe Ruth, New York Yankees	47	1968	Frank Howard, Washington Senators	44
1927	Babe Ruth, New York Yankees	60	1969	Harmon Killebrew, Minnesota Twins	49
1928	Babe Ruth, New York Yankees	54	1970	Frank Howard, Washington Senators	44
1929	Babe Ruth, New York Yankees	46	1971	Bill Melton, Chicago White Sox	33
1930	Babe Ruth, New York Yankees	49	1972	Dick Allen, Chicago White Sox	37
1931	Babe Ruth, New York Yankees	46	1973	Reggie Jackson, Oakland A's	32
	Lou Gehrig, New York Yankees	46	1974	Dick Allen, Chicago White Sox	32
1932	Jimmie Foxx, Philadelphia Athletics	58	1975	George Scott, Milwaukee Brewers	36
1933	Jimmie Foxx, Philadelphia Athletics	48		Reggie Jackson, Oakland A's	36
1934	Lou Gehrig, New York Yankees	49	1976	Graig Nettles, New York Yankees	32
1935	Hank Greenberg, Detroit Tigers	36	1977	Jim Rice, Boston Red Sox	39
	Jimmie Foxx, Philadelphia Athletics	36	1978	Jim Rice, Boston Red Sox	46
1936	Lou Gehrig, New York Yankees	49	1979	Gorman Thomas, Milwaukee Brewers	45
1937	Joe DiMaggio, New York Yankees	49	1980	Ben Oglivie, Milwaukee Brewers	41
1938	Hank Greenberg, Detroit Tigers	46		Reggie Jackson, New York Yankees	41
1939	Jimmie Foxx, Boston Red Sox	35	1981	Eddie Murray, Baltimore Orioles	22
1940	Hank Greenberg, Detroit Tigers	41		Tony Armas, Oakland A's	22
1941	Ted Williams, Boston Red Sox	37		Dwight Evans, Boston Red Sox	22
1942	Ted Williams, Boston Red Sox	36		Bobby Grich, California Angels	22

HOME TEAM. The team on whose grounds the game is played. By tradition the home team bats last, which is considered to be an advantage.

HOOK. Another name for a curveball. Also used to describe what a manager does to a pitcher in trouble: he comes out and gives him the hook.

HOP. A sudden rise taken by a pitch, usually a fastball. Also, the bounce of the ball. A grounder takes a bad hop when the infielder doesn't catch it, or a good one when he does.

HORNSBY, ROGERS. There's plenty of room for argument over who is baseball's greatest player ever, but from 1921 to 1925 there's little doubt the game's greatest hitter was Rogers Hornsby, St. Louis Cardinal second baseman.

Hornsby, born on April 27, 1896, in Winters, Texas, won five National League batting titles over that five-year period, hitting .397, .401, .384, .424, and .403. He also won the batting title in 1920 with .370 and again in 1928 when he hit .387 with the Boston Braves.

The Rajah (a play on "Roger") played for five teams—the Cardinals, Giants, Cubs, Braves, and St. Louis Browns—and managed five, including the 1926 National League champion St. Louis Cardinals, whom he led as player-manager to the world championship. His .358 lifetime average is second only to Ty Cobb's, and he hit 301 homers. Elected to the Hall of Fame in 1942, Hornsby died in 1963.

HOT CORNER. Third base, so called because of the hot shots hit at the third baseman. Third base is also called the far turn or far corner.

HOT DOG. Not only the kind you put mustard on, but also a player who, the opposition believes, is showing off for the fans or the television camera. A leading hot dog is Reggie Jackson, and going back a few years there was none like Vic Power, a Fancy Dan first baseman who had the habit of catching every ball with one hand. Because Power was a Spanish-speaking native of Puerto Rico, hot dog was translated into *perro caliente* for his and his followers' benefit.

HOT-STOVE LEAGUE. Fan-to-fan baseball conversation, discussion, or argument during the winter, so called because of the custom of a group of men sitting around a pot-bellied stove in the local general store to talk baseball.

HOUSTON ASTROS. The Astros went into the final weekend of the 1980 season knowing that all they needed for their first divisional championship was one victory. What they didn't know was how hard it would be to get. After losing three straight games to the Dodgers to force a one-game playoff, the Astros finally had their moment of glory.

With Joe Niekro pitching masterfully and Art Howe contributing a home run, the Astros blasted the Dodgers, 7–1, to wrap up the National League West title. They eventually lost the championship series to the Phillies in five dramatic games, but that could not overshadow the tremendous steps the team had made.

73•

• *When the National League Championship Series was held in 1980 between Houston and Philadelphia, it marked the first post-season play ever in the Houston Astrodome.*

When Houston joined the league in 1962, the owners were determined the team would be called the Houston Colt 45s—guns, not horses. But everyone called them the Houston Colts—horses, not guns. And in their early years a lot of people called them patsies. The team, like all new teams, didn't win too often.

In 1964 they became the Astros when they moved to baseball's first indoor stadium, the plush Astrodome. By the late sixties the emergence of stars like Rusty Staub, Larry Dierker, and Don Wilson made the Astros respectable. In 1967 the Astros had their first home-grown power hitter in

Jimmy Wynn, the Toy Cannon, who blasted 37 homers and knocked in 107 runs that season.

It wasn't until 1979, though, that the Astros started repaying their opponents for all those early-day defeats. Pitcher J.R. Richard, reliever Joe Sambito, outfielders Cesar Cedeno and Jose Cruz, and infielder Enos Cabell kept the team in contention right to the wire.

The signing of free agent Nolan Ryan enabled the Astros to withstand the loss of Richard, who suffered a stroke in the summer of 1980. The Astros had come a long way from the days of the Colt 45s.

HUBBELL, CARL. Carl Hubbell had been a starting pitcher for the New York Giants since 1928, pitching a no-hitter in 1929 against the Pirates and an incredible 18-inning, complete-game shutout against the Cardinals in 1933. But he had never had to face the kind of lineup he was up against as he took the mound to start the 1934 All-Star Game for the National League.

The lineup was awesome, with Babe Ruth, Lou Gehrig, Jimmie Foxx, Al Simmons, and Joe Cronin, all future Hall of Famers. But the Carthage, Missouri, native was up to the task, striking out all five in a row in one of baseball's greatest pitching exhibitions ever.

Hubbell wound up with 253 career wins, all with the Giants, including five 20-game seasons. He was elected to the Hall of Fame in 1947.

INFIELD. The territory including the four bases and that area within it, although there is no strict ruling on where the infield ends and the outfield begins. Sometimes called the diamond because the infield is shaped like a diamond with the distance from home to second being greater than from home to first, home to third, or first to third. The infield is also the all-inclusive term for the four infielders—the first baseman, second baseman, third baseman, and shortstop.

INFIELDER. One who mans a defensive position in the infield. The first baseman, second baseman, third baseman, and shortstop are generally thought of as a team's infielders, although, technically, the pitcher and catcher are also members of the infield.

INFIELD FLY. A fair fly ball (not a line drive or bunt) that can be caught by an infielder with ordinary effort, when first and second bases or first, second, and third bases are occupied before two are out. The umpire simply says "Infield fly" and the batter is automatically out whether the ball is caught or not. This is for the protection of the runners, who may advance at their own risk.

INFIELD HIT. A base hit, usually a grounder, that is not hit beyond the infield. Often called a bleeder or scratch hit.

INNING. That part of a game within which the teams alternate on offense and defense and in which there are three put-outs for each team. Each team's time at bat is a half-inning, and a regulation game consists of nine full innings, although a game will go longer if the score is tied after nine innings.

INTENTIONAL WALK. Deliberate, strategic base on balls. The pitcher throws so wide that the batter has little chance of reaching the pitch. Unpopular with fans, the intentional walk is standard practice in certain situations, most commonly in the late innings of a close game. If second base is occupied and first is not, a dangerous batter may be walked in hope of setting up a double play or a force play. An intentional walk is usually a sign of respect for the batter. In 1969 Willie McCovey of the San Francisco Giants received 45 intentional walks, and Roger Maris of the New York Yankees received 4 intentional walks in one 12-inning game in 1962.

INTERFERENCE. The act of obstructing a play. Interference may be caused by the offense (getting in the way of a fielder attempting to make a play), defense (preventing a batter from hitting at a pitched ball), umpire (hindering a catcher's throw or being hit with a batted ball), or a spectator (reaching out of the stands to touch a live ball). On any interference the ball is dead, and all runners must return to the last base that was, in the judgment of the umpire, legally touched at the time of interference unless otherwise provided by the rules.

IN THE HOLE. A pitcher is in the hole when he is behind by at least two pitches—two balls and no strikes, three balls and no strikes, three balls and one strike. It also means the territory to the shortstop's right and the second baseman's left or any other normally unguarded territory. If the shortstop or second baseman goes into the hole to throw a man out, it's an exceptionally good play.

IRON MAN. A player who rarely leaves a game, playing despite minor injuries. Some examples are Iron Man Joe McGinnity, a New York Giant pitcher soon after the turn of the century who often pitched two games in one day; and first baseman Lou Gehrig of the New York Yankees, who played in a record 2,130 games in a row. Outfielder Billy Williams holds the National League Iron Man record, having played in 1,117 games in a row when he was with the Chicago Cubs.

IRON MIKE. Automatic pitching device. Such machines have been experimented with since 1896, but they did not come into practical use until Branch Rickey, as president of the Brooklyn Dodgers, used them for batting practice in training camps after World War II. Now Iron Mike has been perfected to such a point that he can deliver just about every kind of pitch except a spitball. He is the coolest pitcher of them all, he does not need three days' rest between starts, and he never complains about a sore arm or breaks training.

● *Although Iron Mike occasionally needs some oil, he is one pitcher whose arm never tires.*

● *Power-hitter Reggie Jackson made for an ongoing soap opera at Yankee Stadium.*

JACKSON, REGGIE. Reggie Jackson cocked his bat, waiting for the pitch like a coiled snake sizing up its prey. This was the 1977 World Series, and Jackson was turning it into a one-man show. He had already hit four home runs, two of them on consecutive first-pitch swings in the sixth game. Now he was at the plate again and Yankee Stadium was a sea of sound as more than 55,000 fans roared in anticipation.

Sure enough, Jackson swung at the first pitch again, and this time he sent a towering drive into an unoccupied area of the bleachers, his third straight homer and his fifth of the Series, writing his name in the record books with an exclamation point next to it.

The only other man to hit three homers in a single World Series game was the legendary Babe Ruth, and no one—not even Ruth—ever hit five homers in a single Series.

The power show earned Jackson the 1977 Series MVP award and capped a soap opera season for the slugger, who had signed a $2.9 million free-agent contract with the Yankees in November 1976. Jackson quarreled with manager Billy Martin and some teammates who resented his style. But there could be no quarrel about his performance. He averaged 32 home runs for each of his first four seasons in New York and soared past 400 homers for his career.

Before joining the Yankees, Reggie helped Oakland to three straight world championships—he. was also World Series MVP in 1973. And after signing with New York, Jackson played in three more Series. His post-season batting exploits earned him the nickname "Mr. October."

Jackson was born on May 18, 1946, in Wyncote, Pennsylvania, and was a four-sport star in high school before moving on to

Arizona State. In two years there he broke all of the school's home-run records. Then Jackson signed a bonus contract with Charlie Finley's Oakland A's, starting a major-league career that has had its peaks and valleys but has never been dull.

JAMMED. A batter says he was jammed when he's been pitched close (the intention being to restrict his swing, not hit him).

JOCKEY. A player who rides the opposition with taunts. He is often called a bench jockey because he heckles chiefly from the dugout. It is an art and a vital part of the tradition of the game. The taunts are designed to disturb, upset, and break the concentration of a rival player, and they are usually given and taken in good spirit, but occasionally they cause ill feelings. It is legend that in the 1932 World Series the Chicago Cubs so annoyed Babe Ruth with their bench jockeying that in the fifth inning of the third game Ruth deliberately took two strikes from pitcher Charley Root, then pointed to the most distant part of Wrigley Field and hit the next pitch right where he had pointed.

JOHNSON, WALTER. When Walter Johnson was 14 in 1901, he moved with his family from Humboldt, Kansas, to California, where his father hoped to strike it rich in the oil fields.

No oil came the Johnsons' way, but their son did start playing baseball for oil company teams, where he was discovered by a traveling salesman scouting for the Washington Senators. Things were never the same for the Johnsons.

From 1907 to 1927 Johnson was the Senators' top pitcher. He won 20 or more games a season 12 times, including an American League high 36 in 1913. In 21 seasons the Big Train (so called because the speed of his fastball was said to match that of a roaring locomotive) won 416 games, second only to Cy Young. Johnson still holds the record for most career strikeouts with 3,503. In 1936 he joined Babe Ruth, Honus Wagner, Ty Cobb, and Christy Mathewson as original Hall of Famers. He died in 1946.

JUNK MAN. Term applied, not necessarily with disparagement, to a pitcher who relies on off-speed pitches and tricks instead of a fastball. It was first applied to Ed Lopat of the Yankees and then to Stu Miller of the Baltimore Orioles.

Garry Schumacher, public relations director of the San Francisco Giants, once described Miller's fastball as the Wells Fargo pitch—"It comes to you in easy stages."

Dusty Rhodes of the Giants said of Miller: "He's the only pitcher I ever saw who changes speeds on his changeup."

The most famous remark concerning Stu Miller, the junk man, is that he had three speeds—slow, slower, and slowest.

KALINE, AL. One of the few major-league players who never played in the minor leagues, Al Kaline was the youngest player ever to win the American League batting title when he hit .340 for the Detroit Tigers before his twenty-first birthday.

Kaline, born in Baltimore on December 19, 1934, missed 400 homers by just one, and reached the coveted 3,000-hit mark before retiring in 1974 after 22 seasons. He was one of baseball's best right fielders, with great speed and an excellent arm.

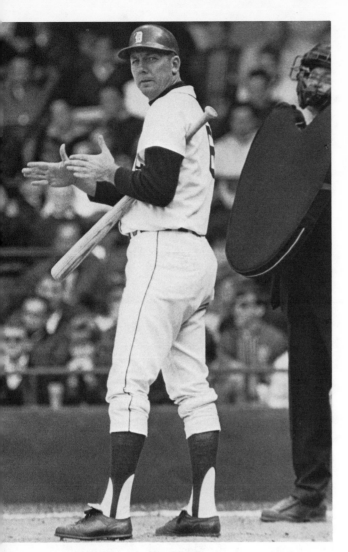

• *Al Kaline was Mr. Tiger.*

Yankees' Rich Gossage was pitching to the Royals' George Brett in the seventh inning of the third game of the 1980 American League championship series. The Royals had won the first two games in Kansas City and were hoping to wipe out the sting of being eliminated by the Yankees in three previous playoffs.

The Royals were trailing in the third game, 2–1, when Brett came to bat with two runners on. Gossage threw, Brett swung, and over 56,000 fans in Yankee Stadium groaned. The ball soared high into the upper deck in right field, giving the Royals a 4–2 win and their first pennant in the club's 12-year history.

It was fitting that Brett was the hero, since he had excited the baseball world all summer as he tried to become the first man since Ted Williams (in 1941) to bat .400 in a season. A late-season slump and injuries deprived Brett of the honor, and he finished at .390.

Though the Royals eventually lost the World Series to Philadelphia in six games,

In 1980 Kaline became only the tenth man in baseball history to win election to the Hall of Fame his first time on the ballot. He has been a broadcaster since retiring.

• *The Royals' Willie Wilson douses George Brett with champagne after Kansas City won the American League West championship in 1980.*

KANSAS CITY ROYALS. It was baseball at its classic best: a great fastball pitcher facing a great fastball hitter. The

the club's future as a contender was certain.

Forgotten were the early days of 1969 and 1970 when the franchise lost 190 games in its first two seasons. And forgotten, too, were all those playoff losses to the Yankees.

KEYSTONE. Second base, so called because it is often the scene of the most important action in the infield. The shortstop and second baseman make up the keystone combination.

KILLEBREW, HARMON. Wide-shouldered and strong as a lumberjack, Harmon Killebrew had the facility for clouting baseballs tremendous distances.

A native of Payette, Idaho, where he was born on June 29, 1936, he was signed by the Washington Senators in 1954, launching a 22-year career in which he would hit 573 home runs, the most ever produced by a right-handed batter in the American League.

• *Mighty Harmon Killebrew walloped 573 home runs.*

On six occasions he either led or tied for the league lead in homers; eight times he belted 40 or more and nine times he had more than 100 RBI's.

Initially signed as a second baseman, Harmon played first, third, and the outfield for the Senators (who became the Minnesota Twins in 1961), and was a designated hitter for the Kansas City Royals.

He played in 11 All-Star Games and was the American League's Most Valuable Player in 1969.

KNOTHOLE GANG. In baseball's earliest days, youngsters who couldn't afford a ticket would watch a game by peeping through knotholes in the wooden fences. After World War II some major-league teams, in a promotional effort, organized knothole gangs made up of kids who got in free or received cut-rate tickets.

KNUCKLEBALL. A pitch thrown by gripping the ball with the fingernails, fingertips, or knuckles and thrown with little effort. It is used as an off-speed pitch and is usually acted on by air currents or wind, which make the ball react in a strange manner. The pitcher rarely knows how the ball will break, so it is a difficult ball to catch or to hit. It is also difficult to throw effectively. The leading pitcher of the knuckleball, butterfly, or flutterball was Hoyt Wilhelm of the New York Giants, Baltimore Orioles, St. Louis Cardinals, and Chicago White Sox. Other outstanding knuckleball pitchers have been Dutch Leonard, Wilbur Wood, and Phil Niekro.

KOUFAX, SANDY. The bus ride was one of dozens that teams take in spring training, crisscrossing Florida to play exhibition games. But it was the most significant ride of Sandy Koufax's life.

earned-run average. Then came 25 victories, 306 strikeouts, and a 1.88 ERA in 1963 when he pitched two of Los Angeles' four World Series victories. He followed that with seasons of 19-5, 26-8, and 27-9 as he often bordered on the unhittable.

There were a then record four no-hitters, including a perfect game; five ERA titles in a row; four strikeout crowns, including a record 382 (since broken by Nolan Ryan) in 1965; and three Cy Young awards.

Hampered by an arthritic elbow, Koufax, who was born December 30, 1935, in Brooklyn, New York, retired at age 30, cutting short a brilliant career that sent him to the Hall of Fame in 1971, the youngest man to win that honor.

● *Dodger Sandy Koufax threw four no-hitters.*

● *Phil Niekro grips the knuckleball that baffles and bewilders.*

Koufax was a talented but erratic left-hander for the Los Angeles Dodgers and had struggled through six mostly average seasons. He was depressed and talked over his trouble with reserve catcher Norm Sherry. The solution they hit on was for the pitcher to ease up on the mound, stop trying to overpower every hitter, and to mix curves and changeups with his explosive fastball.

The formula worked immediately, and from 1961 to 1966 Koufax established one of the most remarkable pitching records in baseball history. He led the National League with 269 strikeouts and posted an 18-13 record in 1961. A circulation problem in his finger limited him to 14-7 the next year, but he led the league with a 2.54

L

LADIES' DAY. A day set aside when women are admitted free or on payment of a service charge and tax. The St. Louis Browns established the custom in 1912. A provision requiring that the ladies have ticket-buying escorts was abandoned when the Browns found themselves running an impromptu dating service as girls gathered outside the gates shopping for escorts.

LAUGHER. Ballplayers' description of a game in which they have such a commanding lead that they can stop worrying. In their first four years the New York Mets had one laugher—when they had a 19–1 lead over the Cubs with two out in the ninth inning. After that game the sports department of a Connecticut newspaper received a call from a fan:

"Is it true the Mets scored nineteen runs today?" asked the fan.

"Yes," said the newspaperman, "it's true."

"Did they win?" asked the fan.

LAY ONE DOWN. To bunt.

LEAD-OFF MAN. Also known as the leading lady. The first batter in the lineup or in any inning. The lead-off man in the lineup is a very important player because he comes to bat more often than anyone else on the team. Because of that, a lead-off man should be an exceptional judge of a pitch and therefore get many bases on balls, or he should be an exceptional hitter with excellent speed.

LEFT FIELD. The outfield territory beyond third base and extending down that line in fair territory, bordered by the area covered by the center fielder. The outfielder who covers left field is the left fielder.

LEFT-HANDER. Left-handers are known as southpaws, portsiders, and, traditionally and affectionately, eccentrics. This applies only to left-handed throwers, particularly pitchers. There is nothing crazy about left-handed batters. In fact, it is something to be desired, even cultivated.

Left-handed hitters have two advantages. First, swinging from the first-base side, they get a head start toward the base and have a better chance of beating out groundballs or double-play relays. Second, the average batter is more effective against a pitcher who throws from his opposite side, giving left-handed swingers another edge, since most pitchers are right-handed.

Many batters, naturally right-handed but bothered by right-handed curveballs, turn left-handed in their youth. This accounts for the fact that while fewer than a fifth of the players who reach the majors are left-handed throwers (and most of these are pitchers), almost a third are left-handed batters.

LINE DRIVE. A hard-hit ball that travels a straight, relatively low course and carries as far as the infielders or farther before bouncing or being caught. Also called a blue dart, screamer, rope, or clothesline. A player who hits a line drive is said to have hung out the clothes.

LINEUP. *See* Batting Order.

LITTLE LEAGUE. In 1939 in the city of Williamsport, Pennsylvania, Carl E. Stotz started the first Little League, made

• *Taiwan pitcher Dai Han-Chao is hoisted in triumph after his team's victory in the 1979 Little League World Series in Williamsport, Pennsylvania.*

ularly Taiwan. Since then only two American teams have won championships—Wayne, New Jersey, in 1970, and Lakewood, New Jersey, in 1975 (when teams from Taiwan were not permitted to compete because of questions about their eligibility).

LIVELY BALL. *See* Ball.

LONG BALL. A ball that is batted deep to the outfield or out of the playing area. A home-run hitter is a long-ball hitter.

LONG MAN. A relief pitcher who comes in early in the game and is expected to pitch five or six innings.

LONG STRIKE. Television commentators' vernacular for a batted ball that travels a long distance but is foul.

LOS ANGELES DODGERS. It was October 6, 1963, and the Dodgers were on the verge of getting revenge. They had taken the first three games of the World Series from their arch-rivals, the Yankees, and were leading the fourth game, 2–1, in the ninth inning.

Seven times previously the Dodgers had won the National League pennant and played the Yankees in the Series; six of those times the Dodgers had failed to win the championship. Their only success against the Yankees had come way back in 1955, when the team was based in Brooklyn. But

up of three teams of neighborhood boys. Its purpose was to provide summer activity. The following year there were four teams in the league, and soon the idea of a Little League began to spread and grow by leaps and bounds.

By 1980 the Little League included millions of boys in thousands of leagues in more than 30 countries. And, thanks in large measure to a court order in 1974, there are girls playing Little League hardball with and against boys. The greatest number, however, are competing in the Little League's softball program, which, interestingly enough, includes boys as well.

The boys' program culminates with the annual Little League World Series in Williamsport, which is official Little League headquarters. Little League has its own rules and regulations, the most basic of which is that no youngster is eligible to compete if he or she will be thirteen years old before August 1 of that year.

Since 1967 the World Series has been dominated by teams from the Orient, partic-

● *They were the Boys of Summer, Brooklyn's Dodgers in the fifties: (left to right) Duke Snider, Gil Hodges, Jackie Robinson, Pee Wee Reese, and Roy Campanella.*

in the 1963 Series Hector Lopez's ground-ball became an easy third out for Maury Wills and the Dodgers had their revenge, a sweep of the hated Yankees. The championship in Los Angeles was celebrated in Brooklyn, too.

The Dodgers' early days in Brooklyn were filled with comedy and failure, although the team did win pennants in 1900, 1916, 1920, and 1941. Crazy things happened in Brooklyn: Casey Stengel tipped his hat and a bird flew out; pitcher Billy Loes lost a groundball in the sun; the Dodgers blew a 13½-game lead in August.

But the team became a powerhouse in the 1950s under Branch Rickey, who in 1946 had signed Jackie Robinson, the first black in organized ball. With such stars as Robinson, Pee Wee Reese, Gil Hodges, Duke Snider, Roy Campanella, Carl Furillo, Don

● *When the Brooklyn Dodgers moved to Los Angeles, their new audience included stars from Hollywood, the television and movie-making capital of the world. Actor Walter Matthau (center), who coached the Bad News Bears in the movie of that name, and comedian Jerry Lewis (right) share a laugh with Steve Garvey of the Dodgers.*

Newcombe, and Preacher Roe, the Dodgers won six pennants between 1947 and 1956.

Although their address changed to Los Angeles in 1958, their taste for winning remained the same—they won the 1959 championship. After winning three pennants in a four-year span, from 1963 to 1966 (with Sandy Koufax and Don Drysdale the stars), the Dodgers hit a drought until 1974, when they started a streak of three pennants in five years. The Dodgers of the seventies (Steve Garvey, Ron Cey, Don Sutton) carried on a tradition that had its roots on another shore. It was a tradition of winning. And it was continued in the 1981 World Series when the Dodgers beat the Yankees in six games, after losing the first two. Fernando Valenzuela, the Dodgers' sensational 20-year-old rookie pitcher, won the third game.

LOSING PITCHER. The pitcher charged by the official scorer as being the loser of the game. Often referred to simply as the loser. A pitcher is called the loser if he leaves the game with his team trailing and if his team never ties the score.

LOWER HALF. The last half of an inning.

MAGIC NUMBER. Near the end of the season, newspapers begin printing the magic number, which shows how many games the leading team must win and how many games any other team must lose for the leader to clinch the pennant. Getting smaller as the victories and defeats add up,

the magic number dramatizes the approaching end of the race.

To determine a magic number, start with two teams: Team A has won the most games so far and Team B is any other team. Add the number of games Team B has won to the number of games it still has to play. From that amount subtract the number of games Team A has won. Add 1 to that number and you have the magic number, the number that will eliminate Team B.

For example, assume the Minnesota Twins have won 93 and lost 59. The Chicago White Sox have won 89 and lost 63. The schedule consists of 162 games, leaving both teams with 10 games to play. Add the number of White Sox victories (89) to their games remaining (10). Subtract the number of Minnesota victories (93), then add 1. The result is 7, the magic number. Thus, as long as the Twins win seven more games, they will beat out the White Sox in the pennant race.

Stated more simply, the idea is to see how many victories the trailing team would have if it won all its remaining games, and how many victories the leading team would need to top that. In this example the White Sox could win 99 games at most. The Twins, having won 93, would need 7 victories to top 99.

MAJOR LEAGUE BASEBALL PLAYERS ASSOCIATION. The union (also called MLBPA) of big-league ballplayers. On their behalf it has won several important rulings, including the ending of the reserve clause, which bound a player to the team that owned his contract and prevented him from having a say in any trade. This landmark case, involving pitchers Andy Messersmith and Dave McNally, ushered in the era of the millionaire free agent.

The MLBPA also won the right to salary arbitration. That means when a player and a team can't agree on his salary, an impartial person decides. Each club has a player representative in the MLBPA.

In 1981 the MLBPA, whose leader is Marvin Miller, called a strike against the owners that ran 50 days. It was basically over the issue of free agency and whether a team losing a free agent should receive another player in exchange (compensation). The players claimed that any compensation would hurt their chances for free movement from one team to another, but management insisted that a team losing a free agent must be given a player in return. The strike was finally settled when the two sides agreed on a "pool" compensation plan in which all teams would submit a list of players. A team that loses a free agent will select another player from that list. (*See also* Draft; Free Agent.)

MAJOR LEAGUES. The term applies to the American and National leagues combined. Often called the big leagues or simply the bigs or majors.

MANAGER. The field director of a team, usually not a player, although there have been player-managers, particularly in the minor leagues. He makes all the important decisions, from picking the starting lineup to deciding strategy—bunt? steal? pinch-hit? replace the pitcher? He also keeps in close touch with the head of the team's farm system so that a player doing well in the minors can be tapped to fill in as needed. Players traditionally call the manager Skipper or Skip to his face and the Old Man or worse behind his back. In print the manager may be the pilot, boss, boss man, or the fearless, peerless, or cheerless leader.

MANTLE, MICKEY. Mickey Mantle brought the bat forward. The crunch of the ball against it had that true, deep sound that told everyone who heard it to watch this one.

It was April 17, 1953, and Mantle was starting his third season with the New York Yankees. Chuck Stobbs was Washington's pitcher, and Mantle connected against him in old Griffith Stadium. The ball soared high and far, but it was no ordinary home run. An enterprising Yankee employee whipped out a tape measure, tracked the ball down, and dutifully reported that Mantle's shot had traveled 565 feet. It was baseball's first tape-measure homer, and it was not Mantle's last.

He came closer than any man in history to hitting a ball out of Yankee Stadium. One of the game's most feared power hitters during the 1950s and 1960s, he threatened to do just that every time he came to bat.

Mantle was born on October 20, 1931, in Spavinaw, Oklahoma, and was not yet 20 years old when he started in right field, next to the immortal Joe DiMaggio, in the 1951 World Series. A year later he took DiMaggio's place as the Yankee center fielder.

A three-time MVP, Mantle won the Triple Crown in 1956 when he batted .353, with 52 homers and 130 RBI's—the best in his league in all three categories. He finished his career with 536 homers, 1,509 RBI's, and a ticket to the Hall of Fame.

MARIS, ROGER. He will remember the day in a way that nobody else could. It was October 1, 1961, and the pressure on Roger Maris was unbearable. The New York Yankee outfielder swung at a pitch thrown by Tracy Stallard of the Boston Red Sox. It landed in the right-field seats at Yankee Stadium, and it landed Maris in the record book. It was the home run (number 61) that broke Babe Ruth's mark for a single season, which had stood since 1927. (*See* Home Run.)

Maris' 12-year career in the majors took him from Cleveland and Kansas City to New

York before he finished with St. Louis. But for the baseball world, the only year that mattered was the one in which he chased and passed the Babe.

MATHEWS, EDDIE. They played baseball, not polo, at New York's Polo Grounds, home of the New York Giants. And on September 27, 1953, Eddie Mathews came to town with the Boston Braves for a game against the Giants.

He was 21 years old, a rookie third baseman. Once, twice, three times he hit home runs that afternoon, the first rookie ever to do so.

The home run would be a trademark throughout Mathews' 16-year career. He hit 30 or more nine years in a row and wound up with a career total of 512, tenth on the all-time list.

● *Mickey Mantle homers in the 1964 World Series against the Cardinals.*

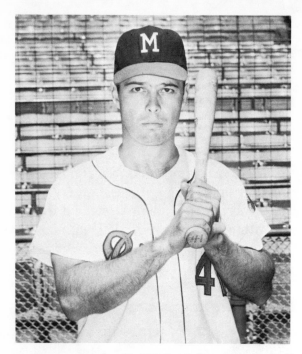

• *Home runs propelled Eddie Mathews into the Hall of Fame.*

Mathews, born on October 13, 1931, in Texarkana, Texas, was an all-star 12 times and played on two Milwaukee Braves' pennant-winning teams. He was the only player ever to play for one team in three different home cities—the Boston, Milwaukee, and Atlanta Braves. He finished with the 1968 world champion Detroit Tigers and made it to the Hall of Fame in 1978, after a brief stint as the Braves' manager.

MATHEWSON, CHRISTY. Win-

ning 30 games in a season is an accomplishment only a handful of major-league pitchers have achieved even once in their careers. Yet in the 17 seasons Christy Mathewson hurled for the New York Giants, the right-hander known as Big Six (because he was six feet tall) topped the magic 30 mark four times, including 1908, when he won a modern National League record 37 games.

Born on August 12, 1880, in Factoryville, Pennsylvania, Mathewson began his major-league career with the New York Giants in 1900. By the time he retired in 1916, he'd won 373 games and had 12 seasons in a row of winning 20 games or more.

Mathewson entered the army at the age of 38 in 1918, and in World War I inhaled poisonous gas which led to his death in 1925. Eleven years later he joined Ty Cobb, Babe Ruth, Honus Wagner, and Walter Johnson in the first group elected to the Hall of Fame.

MAYS, WILLIE. The center fielder

took off with the crack of the bat, turning his back on home plate and running straight toward the bleachers—the deepest part of an oval-shaped ballpark called the Polo Grounds. This was the opening game of the 1954 World Series, and Willie Mays, playing center field for the New York Giants, against

• *Willie Mays was known as the "Say Hey Kid" when he performed all sorts of heroics for the New York Giants.*

the Cleveland Indians, was about to write a memorable chapter of Series history.

With the score tied at 2–2 in the seventh inning, Vic Wertz walloped a huge drive to the deepest part of the park. There seemed no way for Mays to run it down, but somehow the Giant center fielder did just that. He overtook the ball a few steps from the bleachers, catching it with his back to the plate, then wheeled and uncorked a brilliant throw to the infield that kept the two Cleveland runners from advancing. The catch, which triggered a four-game Giant sweep, is considered one of the most brilliant defensive plays in World Series history.

That kind of play was almost routine for Mays, who played center field with a dazzle rarely approached in baseball history. Yet Mays is remembered more for his bat than his glove, because in addition to all his defensive skills he was also one of the top sluggers of his era.

Mays walloped 660 home runs in 22 seasons, third on the all-time list behind Hank Aaron (755) and Babe Ruth (714). But Aaron and Ruth did not have the all-around baseball ability of Mays, who also had 338 stolen bases. Mays finished among the leaders in most offensive departments, ending his career with 1,903 runs batted in, 2,062 runs, and 3,283 hits. He batted over .300 ten times, including seven years in a row, and he had eight straight seasons with at least 100 RBI's. He is one of an elite group of players who hit four home runs in one game. He was the National League's Most Valuable Player in 1954 and again in 1965.

Mays was born on May 6, 1931, in Westfield, Alabama, and was elected to the Hall of Fame in 1979, his first year of eligibility. When he was asked who was the best player he ever saw, Mays was honest. "I was," he said. He got no arguments about that.

MEAT HAND. The hand unprotected by a glove. If a player throws right-handed, that is his meat hand. His left is his glove hand. Meat hand has no connection with meathead, another expression heard around the ballpark.

MILWAUKEE BREWERS. They were known as Bambi's Bombers. And it's true—manager George Bamberger's 1979 Milwaukee Brewers were an explosive team. They were led by Gorman Thomas, who topped the American League with 45 hom-

● *Milwaukee's Cecil Cooper hit .352 in 1980, second in the league to Kansas City's George Brett.*

ers, and such other blasters as Sixto Lezcano, Cecil Cooper, and Ben Oglivie.

The Brewers wound up in second place in the American League's Eastern Division, behind the Baltimore Orioles, a far cry from the early days of a franchise that was born in 1969 in Seattle. The Seattle Pilots lasted only one season before moving to Milwaukee as the Brewers in 1970.

Milwaukee had been without a major-league team since 1966, when the Braves left for Atlanta, and Brewer fans responded enthusiastically even though there was little to cheer about until the late 1970s.

In 1978 Milwaukee turned in its best season up to that point when, with lefty Mike Caldwell, Cooper, and Robin Yount, it won 93 games and finished in third place—only 6½ games behind the first-place Yankees.

Although the Brewers didn't come as close in 1980, almost 2,000,000 fans flocked to County Stadium, where they cheered Cooper, whose .352 batting average was second in the league only to George Brett's .390.

The Brewers had come a long way in ten years.

MINNESOTA TWINS. There was little reason to expect great things from the Minnesota Twins as the 1965 season began. They had finished sixth in the American League the year before, four games under .500. And the cast of players was about the same.

But right from opening day, when the

• *Minnesota's Tony Oliva was American League batting champion in 1964 and 1965.*

Twins defeated the 1964 American League champion New York Yankees, it was obvious that things were different. The hitting had always been there, with Harmon Killebrew, Tony Oliva, Don Mincher, Bob Allison, and others. But this year there was also strong pitching, by 21-game winner Jim (Mudcat) Grant and 18-game winner Jim Kaat. And there was defense, particularly from American League Most Valuable Player Zoilo Versalles at shortstop.

The Twins won the American League pennant by seven games in 1965, and they went the full seven games before losing the World Series to Sandy Koufax and the Los Angeles Dodgers. The pennant was the first since the team moved from Washington, D.C., where it played as the Senators until 1961.

In 1924, under player-manager Bucky Harris (in his first season as manager), the Senators won their first American League title and the World Series, with 20-game winner Walter Johnson leading the way. The following year they won the pennant again but lost the World Series in seven games to the Pittsburgh Pirates. Their last league title in Washington came in 1933 under another player-manager, Joe Cronin. The Senators lost the World Series that year to the Giants, four games to one.

The Twins, who have been owned by various members of the Griffith family for more than 60 years, won back-to-back American League West titles in 1969 and 1970, but lost the championship series to Baltimore both times.

Gone from the team are the stars who made Minnesota history, including Rod Carew, who batted .388 in 1977, and Killebrew, the slugger whose 49 homers in 1969 is the club mark.

MINOR LEAGUES.

Leagues that are of secondary importance to the majors, yet still considered part of the overall structure of the sport. The minor leagues are the training ground for young players—the best players move up to the majors. There have been minor-league teams for almost as long as there have been major-league teams, but it wasn't until Branch Rickey thought up the idea, that minor-league teams became part of the farm system of the majors.

Previously, minor-league teams operated independently. They signed their own players and sold them to the highest bidder when they became in demand. Now every minor-league team is either owned directly by a major-league team or has a working agreement with a major, and more than 90 percent of the minor-league players are owned by the major leagues.

Minor-league teams are distributed among graded classifications: AAA leagues, AA leagues, and rookie leagues. There was a time when there were also B, C, and D leagues. In 1948 there were 59 minor leagues. In 1981 there were only 17. The higher a league's classification, the more skilled are the players in that league.

expos

MONTREAL EXPOS. The most memorable pitch in Expos history did not happen in an actual game. It was the ceremonial first toss of Montreal Mayor Jean Drapeau on the opening day of the 1969 season at New York's Shea Stadium. It marked the end of his city's long wait for a major-league baseball franchise.

Though the Expos did win that first game, the franchise's early years were typical of a new team. Playing in tiny Jarry Park, the Expos didn't win many games. But it didn't take long for the club, named after the

● *Behind the plate and at bat, Gary Carter was an explosive force in Montreal.*

city's World's Fair—Expo '67—to win a devoted following. The Expos made a big splash just 10 days into their first season when Bill Stoneman pitched a no-hitter against the Philadelphia Phillies.

Montreal had its share of early heroes. Unquestionably the most popular was Rusty Staub, a redheaded outfielder who captured the fans' imagination with his flair and his bat. Staub earned the affectionate nickname Le Grand Orange.

It wasn't until after the Expos' move into spacious, modernistic Olympic Stadium in 1977 that they became a real contender. Thanks to Steve Rogers, the team's best pitcher, and young power hitters Gary Carter, Andre Dawson, and Ellis Valentine, all products of their farm system, the Expos battled Pittsburgh until the 1979 season's final weekend.

In 1980, when Ron LeFlore stole 97 bases, Montreal again made it close before bowing to the Phillies on the next-to-last day of the season. In 1981 the Expos made it to the National League championship series, losing to Los Angeles in five games.

MOP-UP MAN. A pitcher used late in the game when the outcome of the game is no longer in doubt.

MOUND. Also called the hill. The raised portion of the infield, 15 inches high at its highest point. The pitcher takes his position on a rectangular plate, known as the slab or rubber, set into the top of the mound.

MOVIES. Hollywood producers have been casting their stars in baseball movies from the earliest silent pictures (1908, *Baseball Fan*) to today's made-for-TV films. Even President Ronald Reagan once appeared in a baseball movie—as Hall of Famer Grover

• *Jimmy Stewart and June Allyson starred in* **The Monty Stratton Story.**

• *Ronald Reagan played the role of Grover Cleveland Alexander in* **The Winning Team.** *He's with Mrs. Alexander.*

Cleveland Alexander (1952, *The Winning Team*).

Here is a list of baseball films for those days and nights when the games are rained out:

Baseball Films and Their Stars

Pride of the Yankees—Gary Cooper,
Teresa Wright, Walter Brennan

The Bad News Bears—Walter Matthau,
Tatum O'Neal

Casey at the Bat—Wallace Beery, Sterling Holloway

The Jackie Robinson Story—Jackie Robinson,
Ruby Dee

Whistling in Brooklyn—Red Skelton,
Ann Rutherford

The Winning Team—Ronald Reagan, Doris Day,
Frank Lovejoy

Warming Up—Richard Dix, Jean Arthur

The Monte Stratton Story—James Stewart,
June Allyson

The Great American Pastime—Tom Ewell

Safe at Home—Mickey Mantle, Roger Maris,
Don Collier

It Happens Every Spring—Ray Milland,
Jean Peters, Paul Douglas

Damn Yankees—Tab Hunter, Ray Walston,
Gwen Verdon

Rhubarb—Ray Milland, Jan Sterling

Take Me Out to the Ball Game—Frank Sinatra,
Gene Kelly, Jules Munshin

Bang the Drum Slowly—Robert DeNiro,
Michael Moriarty

The Kid from Left Field—Dan Dailey,
Lloyd Bridges, Anne Bancroft

Over the Fence—Harold Lloyd, Bebe Daniels

The Pinch Hitter—Charles Ray

Kill the Umpire—William Bendix, Una Merkel

The Pride of St. Louis—Dan Dailey, Joanne Dru

The Big Leaguer—Edward G. Robinson,
Jeff Richards, Vera-Ellen

Angels in the Outfield—Paul Douglas,
Keenan Wynn, Janet Leigh

It Happened in Flatbush—Lloyd Nolan

Alibi Ike—Joe E. Brown

Elmer the Great—Joe E. Brown

Ladies Day—Eddie Albert

Fear Strikes Out—Tony Perkins, Karl Malden,
Norma Moore

One Touch of Nature—John Bennett,
John McGraw

Stepping Fast—Tom Mix

Baseball Madness—Gloria Swanson

Babe Comes Home—Babe Ruth, Anna Q. Nilsson

Speedy—Harold Lloyd, Babe Ruth

The Babe Ruth Story—William Bendix,
Claire Trevor, Charles Bickford

Slide, Kelly, Slide—William Haines, Harry Carey,
Sally O'Neil

One in a Million—LeVar Burton, Madge Sinclair,
Billy Martin

● *Paul Winfield, in wheelchair, was Roy Campanella in* It's Good to Be Alive, *the television special based on the life of the former Dodger.*

MURDERERS' ROW. Name given to the 1927 Yankees, considered to be the greatest hitting team ever assembled. There was no weak hitter on the team, which won 110 games led by Babe Ruth's 60 home runs and Lou Gehrig's 47 at a time when home runs were relatively rare.

MUSIAL, STAN. He was coiled in the batter's box like a human corkscrew. It seemed like an impossible position for a hitter to swing from, but Stan Musial managed.

He swung his bat like a magic wand with a precision that made him one of the most feared hitters of his time. He was so good that his last name didn't matter. He was simply Stan the Man.

Musial was born in Donora, Pennsylvania,

● *Stan Musial was one of the best hitters in history, a three-time Most Valuable Player.*

on November 21, 1920, and began his career as a pitcher. But he was such a good hitter that his manager used him in the outfield when he wasn't pitching. One day, while playing the outfield, he fell on his arm. That was the end of his pitching career and the start of one of the greatest hitting careers in major-league history.

Musial came up with the St. Louis Cardinals in 1941 and, except for one year out for military service, remained with the club until 1963. He won seven batting championships, the last one in 1957 when he was 37 years old.

He was voted the Most Valuable Player three times, and he hit .300 in 17 of his 21 full seasons. A veteran of 20 All-Star Games in a row, he holds the record for most homers (6) hit in an All-Star Game.

He walloped 475 career homers among the 3,630 hits that make him fourth on the all-time list behind Ty Cobb, Hank Aaron, and Pete Rose.

Left-handed Stan played outfield and first base. Naturally, he was an overwhelming choice for the Hall of Fame in 1969, his first year of eligibility.

MVP. Short for Most Valuable Player, chosen each year in both major leagues by a committee of baseball writers. The practice of honoring outstanding players began in 1911, when the manufacturers of Chalmers automobiles presented a car to the leading player in each league.

The Chalmers Award was eventually replaced by the league awards, sponsored by the two major leagues but with the provision in the American League that there be no repeaters. Thus Babe Ruth, when he hit 60 homers in 1927, was not eligible because he had won it before. Lou Gehrig was named instead.

The league awards were abandoned after 1929, and the MVP award, sponsored by the Baseball Writers' Association, has been voted annually since 1931. There is no rule against winning it more than once. In fact, several players have won it three times.

● *Most Valuable Players: Milwaukee Braves' Warren Spahn (left) with Cy Young Award and teammate Hank Aaron as the National League's MVP in 1957*

MVP

	NATIONAL LEAGUE		AMERICAN LEAGUE
Year	Player, Club	Year	Player, Club
1931	Frank Frisch, St. Louis Cardinals	1931	Lefty Grove, Philadelphia Athletics
1932	Chuck Klein, Philadelphia Phillies	1932	Jimmie Foxx, Philadelphia Athletics
1933	Carl Hubbell, New York Giants	1933	Jimmie Foxx, Philadelphia Athletics
1934	Dizzy Dean, St. Louis Cardinals	1934	Mickey Cochrane, Detroit Tigers
1935	Gabby Hartnett, Chicago Cubs	1935	Hank Greenberg, Detroit Tigers
1936	Carl Hubbell, New York Giants	1936	Lou Gehrig, New York Yankees
1937	Joe Medwick, St. Louis Cardinals	1937	Charley Gehringer, Detroit Tigers
1938	Ernie Lombardi, Cincinnati Reds	1938	Jimmie Foxx, Boston Red Sox
1939	Bucky Walters, Cincinnati Reds	1939	Joe DiMaggio, New York Yankees
1940	Frank McCormick, Cincinnati Reds	1940	Hank Greenberg, Detroit Tigers
1941	Dolph Camilli, Brooklyn Dodgers	1941	Joe DiMaggio, New York Yankees
1942	Mort Cooper, St. Louis Cardinals	1942	Joe Gordon, New York Yankees
1943	Stan Musial, St. Louis Cardinals	1943	Spud Chandler, New York Yankees
1944	Marty Marion, St. Louis Cardinals	1944	Hal Newhouser, Detroit Tigers
1945	Phil Cavaretta, Chicago Cubs	1945	Hal Newhouser, Detroit Tigers
1946	Stan Musial, St. Louis Cardinals	1946	Ted Williams, Boston Red Sox
1947	Bob Elliott, Boston Braves	1947	Joe DiMaggio, New York Yankees
1948	Stan Musial, St. Louis Cardinals	1948	Lou Boudreau, Cleveland Indians
1949	Jackie Robinson, Brooklyn Dodgers	1949	Ted Williams, Boston Red Sox
1950	Jim Konstanty, Philadelphia Phillies	1950	Phil Rizzuto, New York Yankees
1951	Roy Campanella, Brooklyn Dodgers	1951	Yogi Berra, New York Yankees
1952	Hank Sauer, Chicago Cubs	1952	Bobby Shantz, Philadelphia Athletics
1953	Roy Campanella, Brooklyn Dodgers	1953	Al Rosen, Cleveland Indians
1954	Willie Mays, New York Giants	1954	Yogi Berra, New York Yankees
1955	Roy Campanella, Brooklyn Dodgers	1955	Yogi Berra, New York Yankees
1956	Don Newcombe, Brooklyn Dodgers	1956	Mickey Mantle, New York Yankees
1957	Hank Aaron, Milwaukee Braves	1957	Mickey Mantle, New York Yankees
1958	Ernie Banks, Chicago Cubs	1958	Jackie Jensen, Boston Red Sox
1959	Ernie Banks, Chicago Cubs	1959	Nellie Fox, Chicago White Sox
1960	Dick Groat, Pittsburgh Pirates	1960	Roger Maris, New York Yankees
1961	Frank Robinson, Cincinnati Reds	1961	Roger Maris, New York Yankees
1962	Maury Wills, Los Angeles Dodgers	1962	Mickey Mantle, New York Yankees
1963	Sandy Koufax, Los Angeles Dodgers	1963	Elston Howard, New York Yankees
1964	Ken Boyer, St. Louis Cardinals	1964	Brooks Robinson, Baltimore Orioles
1965	Willie Mays, San Francisco Giants	1965	Zoilo Versalles, Minnesota Twins
1966	Roberto Clemente, Pittsburgh Pirates	1966	Frank Robinson, Baltimore Orioles
1967	Orlando Cepeda, St. Louis Cardinals	1967	Carl Yastrzemski, Boston Red Sox
1968	Bob Gibson, St. Louis Cardinals	1968	Dennis McLain, Detroit Tigers
1969	Willie McCovey, San Francisco Giants	1969	Harmon Killebrew, Minnesota Twins
1970	Johnny Bench, Cincinnati Reds	1970	Boog Powell, Baltimore Orioles
1971	Joe Torre, St. Louis Cardinals	1971	Vida Blue, Oakland A's
1972	Johnny Bench, Cincinnati Reds	1972	Dick Allen, Chicago White Sox
1973	Pete Rose, Cincinnati Reds	1973	Reggie Jackson, Oakland A's
1974	Steve Garvey, Los Angeles Dodgers	1974	Jeff Burroughs, Texas Rangers
1975	Joe Morgan, Cincinnati Reds	1975	Fred Lynn, Boston Red Sox
1976	Joe Morgan, Cincinnati Reds	1976	Thurman Munson, New York Yankees
1977	George Foster, Cincinnati Reds	1977	Rod Carew, Minnesota Twins
1978	Dave Parker, Pittsburgh Pirates	1978	Jim Rice, Boston Red Sox
1979	Keith Hernandez, St. Louis Cardinals	1979	Don Baylor, California Angels
	Willie Stargell, Pittsburgh Pirates	1980	George Brett, Kansas City Royals
1980	Mike Schmidt, Philadelphia Phillies	1981	Rollie Fingers, Milwaukee Brewers
1981	Mike Schmidt, Philadelphia Phillies		

NATIONAL LEAGUE. The older of baseball's two major leagues, the other being the American League. Sometimes called the senior circuit. The National League began in 1876 and represented a rebellion against the establishment of the day, the National Association.

Early in the 1875 season, owners of the Chicago franchise, weary of constant failure, offered the team's presidency to William A. Hulbert, a successful businessman and rabid fan of the Chicago White Stockings. Hulbert asked for a few weeks to consider the offer.

When the champion Boston club visited Chicago, Hulbert met with A.G. Spalding, the league's outstanding pitcher. Hulbert begged Spalding to join him in Chicago. When Hulbert promised Spalding a huge contract for the 1876 season, Spalding agreed to come to Chicago the following year. What's more, Spalding helped Hulbert

sign his teammates Ross Barnes, Cal McVey, and Deacon Jim White, three of the outstanding players in the National Association.

The deal was not supposed to be announced until after the 1875 season, but it leaked out before the season ended, to the embarrassment of Spalding and his friends.

Now there were rumors that Spalding and the other club jumpers might be expelled from the National Association following the 1875 season, making it impossible for them to fulfill their contracts with Hulbert and the White Stockings. Spalding told Hulbert of his fears, and it gave Hulbert an idea. He decided to form a new league. He even had a name. Instead of the National Association of Base Ball Players, he would call his new league the National League of Professional Base Ball Clubs.

Hulbert had a formal constitution drawn up, and then he called officials of the St. Louis, Cincinnati, and Louisville clubs to a secret meeting. He told them of his plan and got a strong vote of confidence. Now he had four teams in his new league, and the next step was to get some eastern teams represented. Hulbert invited the remaining National Association teams to a conference "on matters of interest to the game at large, with special reference to reformation of existing abuses." His summons was answered by all four eastern teams—Philadelphia, Boston, Hartford, and New York.

Hulbert outlined the evils that were demoralizing the players and fans and charged that the National Association was either unable or unwilling to correct the abuses. He called for a new league and produced the constitution of his National League. He won their complete support, and on April 22, 1876, the National League began play with Boston defeating Philadelphia, 6–5, at Philadelphia, one of eight charter members in the National League.

The National League grew to twelve teams and flourished until 1899, when four teams were dropped. They promptly linked up with an outlaw league and formed the eight-team American League. In 1901, when the American League formally opened play as an eight-team league, teams in the National League included Pittsburgh, Philadelphia, Brooklyn, St. Louis, Boston, Chicago, New York, and Cincinnati.

● *A mannequin representing an early National League player.*

The National League stayed that way until 1953, when the Boston Braves asked for, and received, permission to move to Milwaukee. In 1958 the Brooklyn Dodgers moved to Los Angeles and the New York Giants to San Francisco.

In 1962 the National League expanded to 10 teams—one franchise was awarded to New York and was named the Mets, the other went to Houston and was called the Colt 45s, later the Astros. Players for the two new teams were taken from a pool provided by the eight established teams, and the schedule was expanded from 154 games to 162.

In 1966 the Braves became the first club to move twice, shifting from Milwaukee to Atlanta after much legal action. Expansion came again in 1969, when Montreal and San Diego were admitted to the National League.

With the league expanded to 12 teams, division play was thought up. The Eastern Division of the National League was made up of New York, Philadelphia, Pittsburgh, St. Louis, Chicago, and Montreal. The Western Division included Los Angeles, San Francisco, Houston, San Diego, Cincinnati, and Atlanta.

As in the American League, the winners of each division meet in a best-of-five playoff series to determine which team will represent the National League in the World Series.

NEW YORK METS. The fly ball drifted lazily out toward left field, where Cleon Jones was waiting. Jones went down

• *The pitcher, Tom Seaver, appropriately pours the champagne as the New York Mets celebrate their World Series triumph over the Baltimore Orioles in 1969.*

sprouting good young players like Tug McGraw, Jerry Koosman, and Tom Seaver.

It was the pitching of Seaver and Koosman that drove the Mets in 1969. A 100-to-1 shot in spring training, the Mets stayed close to the Chicago Cubs through the summer and then passed them in early September to win the division by eight games. They then beat the Atlanta Braves in three straight playoff games to win their first pennant. After an opening-game loss in the World Series, the Mets won four straight from the Baltimore Orioles, capping the miracle year.

The Mets remained a contender in the early seventies and won the pennant in 1973 behind Seaver, Koosman, and slugger Rusty Staub. But they lost the World Series to Oakland in seven games.

NEW YORK YANKEES. From Babe Ruth to Joe DiMaggio to Mickey Mantle to Reggie Jackson, the Yankees have stood for baseball excellence since 1921, when they won their first of a record 32 pennants.

Originally known as the Highlanders, the team changed its name in 1912 because "Yankees" fit better in newspaper headlines.

In 1920 owner Jacob Ruppert bought Ruth from the Red Sox for $100,000. Ruth became the greatest bargain in history, leading the Yanks to six pennants between 1921 and 1928. The Babe smashed 60 homers in 1927 and, with Lou Gehrig, formed the core of the famed, feared Murderers' Row.

on one knee, cradled the ball, and the miracle was complete. The New York Mets had won the World Series. It happened on October 16, 1969, and set off a wild celebration in the streets of New York.

Only seven years earlier, in the club's first season, the team was the laughingstock of baseball. With a roster made up of over-the-hill players, the Mets lost 120 of 160 games and finished 60½ games out of first place. Casey Stengel, who had managed the Yankees to championship after championship, was the unfortunate one stuck with the chore of managing this motley crew.

But in 1964 things began to change. A new stadium, Shea, was built in Queens, and the team surpassed the Yankees as the area's favorite. The play on the field didn't improve much, but the farm system started

After Ruth retired, DiMaggio became the best slugger on the team in 1936. Nothing else changed, though: the Yanks kept winning. From 1936 through 1964 they captured 22 pennants and 16 world championships. DiMaggio played a key role in the early titles, then Mantle took over in 1951.

Highlights in the Yankees' fantastic success story include DiMaggio's 56-game hitting streak in 1941, five straight world championships from 1949 through 1953, Don Larsen's perfect game in the 1956 World Series, and Roger Maris' 61 homers in 1961.

The Yankees hit upon hard times in the late 1960s and early 1970s, but new owner George Steinbrenner took over in 1973 and turned the team around. With the coming of the free agent, Steinbrenner opened his checkbook to buy players like Reggie Jackson, Catfish Hunter, and Rich Gossage. They helped the Yanks win five division titles and two world championships from 1976 through 1981.

Steinbrenner was still spending in 1981, when he signed free-agent outfielder Dave Winfield to a 10-year, $15 million contract.

The Yankees have always had heroes, but they've also had notable managers, including Miller Huggins, Joe McCarthy, and Casey Stengel, the most colorful and successful of all. Casey guided the team to 10 pennants and seven world championships in 12 years.

NICKNAMES. Five players named Rhodes or Rhoades have appeared in the big leagues, and all but one were nicknamed Dusty. This illustrates two points about baseball nicknames: they're almost inevitable with certain last names (a Rhodes will be Dusty and a Watters will be Muddy), and they're not noted for their originality.

Some obvious physical characteristic or personality trait is the most common basis for a nickname. Examples include players named Red, Whitey, or Lefty, as well as Dizzy Dean, Bugs Raymond, Sad Sam Jones, Slim Sallee, Fats Fothergill, Stubby Overmire, King Kong Keller, Moose Skowron, Ducky Medwick for his waddling gait, and Hawk for any large-nosed player (or Schnozz, as Ernie Lombardi was dubbed).

Harry Brecheen was the Cat because he looked like a cat in the way he sped off the mound to field, and Harvey Haddix was the Kitten because he looked like Harry Brecheen. Marty Marion was the Octopus because he seemed to be all arms as he fielded a ball at shortstop, and Emil Verban

● *Relief pitcher Rich Gossage jumps for joy into the arms of Thurman Munson after the Yankees won the American League pennant for the third straight time against the Royals in 1978.*

became the Antelope mostly because he was Marion's second-base partner with the St. Louis Cardinals.

Harold Reese became Pee Wee, not just because he was small but because he was once a marble champion (a peewee is a small marble), and Jim Bouton was dubbed Bulldog because of his determination. Cap Peterson got his nickname because his real name was Charles Andrew Peterson and his initials were C.A.P.

Nervous habits lead to nicknames: Jittery Joe Berry, Fidgety Phil Collins, Shuffling Phil Douglas. One of the best of these, coined by columnist Jimmy Cannon, was Hot Potato Hamlin for Luke Hamlin, a pitcher who juggled the ball in the palm of his hand before winding up.

Babe, Rube, Kid, and Doc are baseball nicknames of long standing. Bobo, made famous by Bobo Newsom, is now used less as a nickname than as an insult for any player who is thought of as the manager's pet ("He's the Old Man's bobo").

Many nicknames become famous although their origins are never discovered. Pumpsie Green, whose real name is Elijah, said, "Someday I'll write a book and call it *How I Got the Nickname Pumpsie* and sell it for a dollar, and if everybody who ever asked me that question buys the book, I'll be a millionaire."

Nationalities have produced nicknames like Frenchy Bordagaray, Germany Schaefer, Lou (the Mad Russian) Novikoff, and Shanty Hogan. Years ago almost any American Indian or part-Indian player was known as Chief. Almost half of the Spanish-speaking players are certain to wind up being called Chico. There have been Chico Carrasquel, Chico Fernandez, Chico Salmon, Chico Cardenas, and Chico Ruiz.

Charles Dillon Stengel became Casey because he came from Kansas City (KC), but most nicknames of that variety spring from quaint-sounding home towns: Wahoo Sam Crawford from Wahoo, Nebraska; Pea Ridge Day from a town of that name in Arkansas; and Vinegar Bend Mizell from the thriving metropolis of Vinegar Bend, Alabama.

Another popular source is a player's skill or his record, whether favorable or not. Denton Young threw so hard he became known as Cyclone, later shortened to Cy. Joe Wood, another fireballer, was to win fame as Smokey Joe Wood. Odell Hale was Bad News to the pitchers he clobbered, and then there were Home Run Baker, Sliding Billy Hamilton, and Swish Nicholson (for his repeated practice swings, which fascinated the fans).

Not very flattering, although the recipients didn't seem to mind, were names like Boom Boom Beck, Line Drive Nelson, and Losing Pitcher Mulcahy for pitchers who continually took their lumps, and Rocky for somebody with rocks in his head. Of course, if Rocky's given name happened to be Rocco, you could give him the benefit of the doubt.

There were certain annoying nicknames that were saved for the time and place when their use might have the most painful effect. John McGraw liked Muggsy about as much as he liked an extra-inning defeat, while a player who wanted the rest of the day off might have said to umpire Bill Klem, "Where was that last pitch, Catfish?" In a moment he'd be in the shower.

But Klem is gone, and the name Catfish changed from insult to praise after it became the name by which the millionaire Yankee pitcher James Augustus Hunter was known.

It has been said that Catfish Hunter got his nickname when he was a boy of six. One day Jim was missing. His parents searched frantically for him for hours. When they finally found him that evening, he was at his favorite fishing hole, and he had hauled in a mess of catfish. From that day to this, he has been called Catfish, a story that may simply be a figment of the imagination of Charles O. Finley, Hunter's colorful and controversial former employer at Kansas City and Oakland.

● *This was the scene at the first night game played at Brooklyn's Ebbets Field on June 15, 1938. Cincinnati was the Dodgers' opponent, and Reds pitcher Johnny Vander Meer made history when he threw his second no-hit game in a row.*

NIGHT BALL. Baseball was first played under lights in 1880 at Nantasket Beach near Boston. It didn't come to the major leagues until 1935, when Larry MacPhail staged the first night game, in Cincinnati.

Since then, with one lingering exception, every big-league club has installed lights and has been playing an increasing share of its schedule after dark. The Chicago Cubs are the exception. Owner Phil Wrigley clung to the notion that baseball was meant to be played under the sun.

At first, major-league clubs were limited to seven home night games a season, but the number kept growing until it has reached a point where afternoon games, except on a Saturday, Sunday, or holiday, are rare in most big-league ball parks.

When, in 1971, the Baltimore Orioles and Pittsburgh Pirates played the first World Series game at night in Pittsburgh, baseball was firmly established as a nighttime spectacle.

NINE. A baseball team, so called because there are nine players on a side.

NO-HITTER. A no-hit, no-run game. A game in which the pitcher permits the opposing team no base hits and no runs for the entire game. No-hitters are rare enough to be a special event, but plentiful enough so as not to be freakish. As a typical 10-year period, take the years 1948 to 1957. In all, there were 17 no-hitters during the 10-year

● *The New York Yankees' Don Larsen delivers a third-strike pitch to the Dodgers' Dale Mitchell for the final out in the only perfect game in World Series history. It happened on October 8, 1956.*

span, or almost two per year. In 1951 there were four. In 1965 Sandy Koufax of the Los Angeles Dodgers became the first pitcher to pitch four no-hitters, a feat surpassed by Nolan Ryan of the Houston Astros in 1981.

A perfect game is a no-hitter in which not one batter reaches base safely, either by hit, walk, or error. In a perfect game the pitcher faces the minimum of 27 opposing batters. Obviously, perfect games are rarer than no-hitters. There have been only 11 perfect games in major-league history, the most recent occurring in 1981 when Cleveland's Len Barker threw one against the Toronto Blue Jays.

The most famous perfect game was in 1956, and it was the only perfect game ever pitched in a World Series. Don Larsen, a mediocre pitcher who had won 30 and lost 40 in four big-league seasons, pitched it for the New York Yankees against the Brooklyn Dodgers in the fifth game.

After the game, in the madhouse around Larsen's locker, a rookie reporter asked Don, "Is that the best game you ever pitched?"

OAKLAND A'S. Jim (Catfish) Hunter looked for his sign from catcher Jim Pagliaroni. Minnesota pinch-hitter Rich Reese had already fouled off five straight pitches, and the Oakland pitcher was seeking the final out that would put him in baseball's record books.

Hunter calmly nodded his head and

began his windup. The pitch flew from his right hand. Reese swung hard but hit nothing but air. Hunter had his eleventh strikeout, and more important on this May evening in 1968, he had become the first American League pitcher since 1922 to hurl a regular-season perfect game.

Yet another chapter had been written in the topsy-turvy history of the Philadelphia/Kansas City/Oakland Athletics.

The legacy of the A's began in 1901 when Connie Mack (Cornelius McGillicuddy) became manager of the Philadelphia team in the new American League. Mack, who also owned the team, was Mr. Baseball. He managed it for 50 years, winning five world championships, the last in 1930, when he had such stars as Jimmie Foxx, Al Simmons, Mickey Cochrane, Lefty Grove, and George Earnshaw.

● *Jim (Catfish) Hunter starred for the Oakland A's in three world championship seasons.*

● *The Philadelphia A's $100,000 infield of 1912 (left to right): Stuffy McInnis, Eddie Collins, Jack Barry, and Frank (Home Run) Baker*

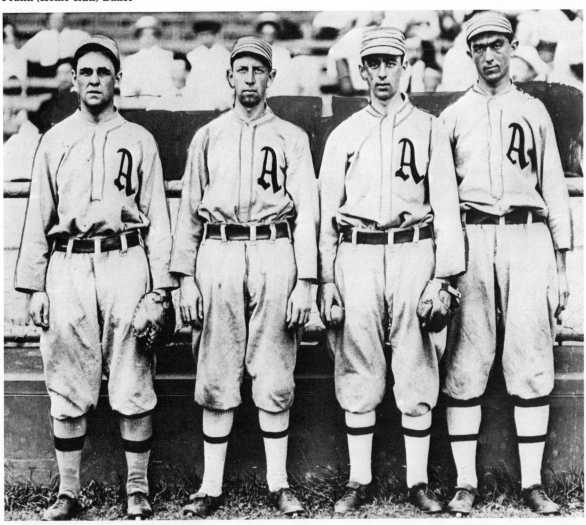

Mack managed his last team in 1950 at the age of 88, living to see the sad day when the A's moved west to Kansas City in 1955. In the course of their stay in Missouri, a colorful, unconventional insurance executive named Charles O. Finley bought the team and changed its location as well as its destiny.

Finley shifted the A's to Oakland in 1968 and, although he fired managers at will, he wound up running the most successful team in the early 1970s. With players like Hunter, Reggie Jackson, Sal Bando, and Vida Blue, the A's strung together three world championships in 1972, 1973, and 1974.

Finley, who once had a mule for a mascot, eventually gave up the mule and sold the team in 1980. But one of his last moves ensured that the team would be as flamboyant as ever; he brought in Billy Martin as manager.

ON DECK. The player waiting to follow the current batter is said to be on deck. According to the rules, he must wait in the on-deck circle, a chalk-marked area placed halfway between home plate and the dugout. The purpose of the on-deck circle is to speed up the game.

ONE O'CLOCK HITTER. It means a batter who is terrific during batting practice (which usually comes an hour before game time), but is a bust during a game. It used to be a two o'clock hitter when games were played at 3 p.m., and sometimes it is a seven o'clock hitter for night games, which start at 8 p.m.

The greatest two o'clock hitter of all time was Tommy Brown, a young wartime infielder for the Brooklyn Dodgers. Brown, who played his first major-league game when he was 16, used to keep complete records of his home runs during batting practice. Each year he would break Babe Ruth's home-run record by June at the latest—in batting practice. However, in 1953, his last year in the major leagues, he hit only two home runs in 65 games for the Chicago Cubs during working hours.

OUT. If you fail to reach first base, you're out. Each team gets three outs an inning. The game is never over until the last man is out. The umpire points his thumb upward to indicate an out.

OUTFIELD. All the area in fair territory beyond the infield and usually bounded by fences or stands. There is no strict dividing mark between the infield and the outfield. The players who cover the three outfield positions—left field, center field, and right field—are called outfielders. One is called the left fielder, one is the center fielder, and one the right fielder, depending on the field he covers. An outfielder is called a gardener, fly chaser, member of the outer garden, outer pasture, or picket patrol; and the entire outfield is often called the picket line.

OUT IN ORDER. A team is out in order, or a pitcher is said to have retired the side in order, if the first three batters in any inning are retired with none reaching base safely.

OUT MAN. An exceptionally weak hitter, sometimes called a lamb, flea hitter, ping hitter, or weak sister. Traditionally the weakest hitter on a team bats eighth. Often he would bat ninth, except that it is considered humiliating to have him bat after the pitcher, usually the poorest hitter on any team. But there are exceptions—it was no disgrace to bat after Don Drysdale of the Los Angeles Dodgers in 1965. An outstanding hitter for a pitcher, Drysdale's batting average that year was higher than that of any regular on the team.

OWNERS. That curious band of monopolists who not only own the baseball teams but run the game, for all practical purposes. They are called the moguls, magnates, and lords of baseball and, in most cases, they do call all the shots. It is the owners who make policy for the game and who approve or disapprove the shifting of a team from one city to another. The owners choose baseball's ranking authority, the commissioner. This sets up a situation in which a man is expected to govern the very men who put him in power.

It used to be that baseball teams were owned by individual citizens whose only interest and only income were the baseball team. That is no longer true. Baseball is now big business, and that is reflected in the ownership of the teams.

For instance, the St. Louis Cardinals are owned by Gussie Busch (Budweiser beer); the Chicago Cubs were owned by the Wrigley family (Wrigley gum) until they were sold in 1981 to the Chicago Tribune Corporation. For many years the owner of the Oakland Athletics was Charles O. Finley, an insurance tycoon. Nobody is sure what the O. stands for, but some believe it was put there by Finley himself, who wanted the world to know that he was an Owner and proud of it.

P

PAIGE, SATCHEL. "Don't look back. Something might be gaining on you."

His words are just part of the legend of pitcher Leroy Robert (Satchel) Paige, baseball's ageless wonder. Prevented from playing in the major leagues until after Jackie Robinson became the first black player to sign with a major-league team, Paige came to the Cleveland Indians in 1948, when, according to a Mobile, Alabama, birth certificate, he was 42 years old.

His major-league record, which includes three scoreless innings for the Kansas City Athletics in 1965 when he was 59, was 28-31, remarkable in view of the fact that he was well past his prime. In the black leagues he regularly recorded 40-victory seasons, and once he struck out 22 major leaguers in an exhibition game. His long overdue election to the Hall of Fame came in 1971.

● *Satchel Paige made his mark with the Kansas City Monarchs in the black leagues long before he got a chance to play in the majors.*

PALMER, JIM. The date was October 6, 1966, and on the mound in Dodger Stadium, Sandy Koufax was making his final start. A storybook finish would have called for at least a shutout by the Dodgers' Hall of Fame left-hander and, indeed, a shutout was pitched in that second game of the 1966 World Series. But it was pitched by a lanky 20-year-old Baltimore right-hander, Jim Palmer, who threw a four-hit shutout. He thus became the youngest pitcher in World Series history to record a shutout.

Palmer was born on October 15, 1945, in New York City, so he was still nine days away from his twenty-first birthday when he pitched that shutout. He had won 15 games that season, but a year later his arm went dead and his career seemed finished. "They told me I would never pitch again," he said.

Determined to work his way back, Palmer spent the next two years pitching in places like Elmira, Rochester, and Miami. Slowly but surely the power returned to his right shoulder, and by 1969 he was back in Baltimore.

Palmer pitched a no-hitter against Oakland that season, compiling a 16-4 record. A year later he achieved the first of eight 20-victory seasons over nine years, stamping himself as one of baseball's top pitchers in the seventies.

• *Jim Palmer has had eight 20-victory seasons.*

PASSED BALL. The catcher's failure to control a pitched ball that should have been controlled with ordinary effort and that results in a base runner advancing. It is also charged as an error to the catcher if a batter reaches first base because of a dropped third strike. There can be no passed ball charged unless there is an advance by a base runner.

PAYOFF PITCH. The pitch that follows a three-ball, two-strike count on the batter. It is so called because, except for a foul ball, this pitch disposes of the batter. A batter who has reached a count of three and two is said to have "run out the string."

PENNANT. The term most commonly used for a league championship. When it is said that the Yankees won the pennant, it means they won the league championship. Less important is the fact that the league champion also receives an actual flag or pennant.

The raising of the championship flag at the beginning of each season is a traditional ceremony in the park of the previous year's league champion. It is a ceremony the Yankees have enjoyed more than any other team. Through 1981 the Yankees had won 33 pennants, almost twice as many as any other club. The pennant winners in the American and National leagues meet each fall in the World Series.

PEPPER. Traditional warm-up game played on the sidelines. One batter and one or more throwers take positions at rather close range, the batter rapping or peppering sharp groundballs to each of the throwers in turn.

PERRY, GAYLORD. His hand moves first across the letters of his uniform. Then he tugs at the bill of his cap. Next his fingers flick across his mouth and then he rubs his hand along the side of his pants. Finally finished with the routine, he often repeats it a second time and maybe even a third. Tug, flick, rub. Clearly, Gaylord Perry is moistening the baseball. The question is where and when.

Perry has been frisked from head to toe on the mound and has driven batters to distraction for years. He has openly confessed to occasionally using baseball's illegal spitball, but the umpires haven't caught him at it yet. Ask him if he still relies on it, and Perry smiles coyly. As long as batters think he does, that's good enough for Perry. Spitballs take off in all directions unpredictably. If a hitter is worried about spitballs, Perry figures it gives the pitcher at least a psychological edge.

Perry, who was born on September 15, 1948, in Williamston, North Carolina, once admitted that he threw a spitball for the first time during a 23-inning marathon game between the San Francisco Giants and the New York Mets. He broke in with the Giants in 1962 and was still pitching in 1981, for the Atlanta Braves. Along the way he'd also

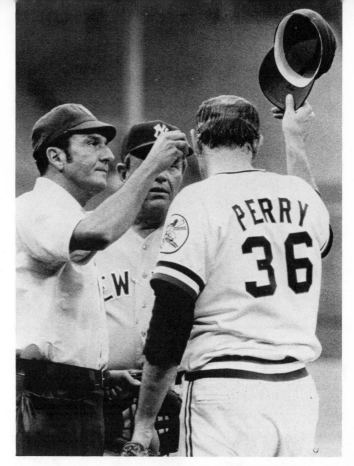

● *Umpire Lou DiMuro checks Gaylord Perry to see if he's using any "greasy kid stuff" when throwing the ball.*

played for Cleveland, Texas, San Diego, and the Yankees.

After the 1981 season, he was just 3 victories short of 300 for his career, and his 3,336 strikeouts were second on the all-time list to Walter Johnson. He was the only pitcher to win the Cy Young Award in both leagues—in 1972 with Cleveland in the American, in 1978 with San Diego in the National.

PHANTOM INFIELD. A stunt drill, occasionally put on before exhibition games, in which a team goes through the motions of infield practice—fungo hitter and all—without a ball.

PHEENOM. Modern lingo for a highly touted rookie. Taken from the word "phenomenon," it was coined by Garry Schumacher, who was public relations director of the New York and San Francisco Giants. He applied it to Clint Hartung, a player with the Giants just after World War II.

Hartung, nicknamed the Hondo Hurricane because he hailed from Hondo, Texas, came to the Giants with such a reputation for versatility and great deeds that the manager's major concern was whether to make him a .400-hitting outfielder or a 30-game winning pitcher. Hartung lasted six years with the Giants, during which time he won 29 games and lost the same number, and had a lifetime batting average of only .212. Since then the term "pheenom" has had a skeptical ring.

PHILADELPHIA PHILLIES. Top of the ninth, two out, bases loaded, Phillies lead the Royals, 4–1, in the sixth game of the 1980 World Series.

Tug McGraw peers down from the mound at KC's Willie Wilson. Black-helmeted riot police and trained attack dogs ring Veterans Stadium, preparing to control the celebration of long-suffering Philadelphia fans. McGraw fires a fastball past Wilson for a third strike and leaps several feet off the ground.

The Phillies, sustained by the arm of Cy Young Award winner Steve Carlton, the bat of Series MVP Mike Schmidt, and the heart of Pete Rose, had finally done it. They'd won their first world championship.

In 1915, behind pitcher Grover Cleveland Alexander, the Phillies won their first pen-nant, only to lose to the Boston Red Sox in the World Series. They didn't win another pennant until Eddie Sawyer's Whiz Kids (all of them under 30) rode a Dick Sisler homer to a final-day clinching of the 1950 flag. But despite a formidable pitching staff that included Robin Roberts and MVP Jim Konstanty, the Whiz Kids were swept by the Yankees in the World Series.

Jim Bunning pitched the first perfect game in the National League in 84 years on June 21, 1964, against the Mets. A stunning, complete collapse of the team in the final two weeks of that season cost the Phillies the pennant.

Rookie manager Dallas Green, a pitcher on the 1961 Phillies team that lost 23 games in a row, led the club out of the wilderness in 1980. The Phils won the division in the final weekend of the season in a head-to-head battle with Montreal, came from behind to beat Houston in the playoffs, and then knocked off the Royals in the World Series.

PICK OFF. To catch a runner off base as the result of a sudden throw from the pitcher or catcher. A good pick-off motion is essential to the success of a pitcher, and therefore many work hard at perfecting their throw to first. It comes naturally to a left-hander, but it is rare that a right-hander has a good pick-off move. An exception is Mike Marshall.

PICK UP. To catch a ball immediately after it hits the ground. Sometimes called trapping a ball or getting it on the short hop.

PINCH-HITTER. One batter substituted for another, so called because he is usually used in a pinch—when there are runners on base late in the game and a hit is needed. Men used as pinch-hitters are often

● *Tug McGraw expresses the glorious moment when his Phillies win the 1980 World Series over the Kansas City Royals.*

players who are not noted for their fielding ability or older players unable to perform at peak efficiency if played daily.

Pinch-hitting is an art, and there have been many successful pinch-hitters. Johnny Frederick, for example, hit six pinch-hit home runs for the Brooklyn Dodgers in 1932. Dave Philley had nine pinch-hits in a row (a record) for the Philadelphia Phillies in 1958 and 1959. The single-season mark is held by Jose Morales, who collected 25 pinch-hits for Montreal in 1976. The all-

time pinch-hit king is Manny Mota, who delivered 150 pinch-hits for various National League teams during nearly twenty years.

PINCH-RUNNER. A runner who substitutes for a teammate who has already reached a base; the original runner is out of the game from that time on. A pinch-runner is used because he is faster than the man on base.

PITCH. A ball delivered to the batter by the pitcher.

PITCHER. The hurler, twirler, flinger, slinger, flipper, chucker, tosser, moundsman. By any name, he's the man who does the throwing.

PITCHERS' DUEL. A close, low-scoring game that is dominated by the pitchers. Praised by old-time baseball fans as those good old pitchers' duels; complained about by modern fans as those boring pitchers' duels.

PITCHER'S RUBBER. A rectangular slab of white rubber 24 inches long and 6 inches wide set in the ground on the pitcher's mound. The pitcher must have his foot on a part of the rubber when he starts his delivery.

PITCHOUT. A pitch delivered wide of the plate on purpose when the catcher suspects that a runner intends to steal. It is thrown wide so the batter cannot reach it and so the catcher will have a clear path for his throw. The penalty for the privilege of throwing a pitchout is that the pitch counts as a ball.

PITTSBURGH PIRATES. The New York Yankees faced the Pirates in the seventh game of the 1960 World Series. The Yankees, winners of 18 previous Series, including a sweep of the Pirates in 1927, had come from behind in the ninth inning to tie the game at 9–9.

The 36,683 fans at Forbes Field were dreading the prospect of extra innings.

Leading off the bottom of the ninth, Pittsburgh's Bill Mazeroski hit Ralph Terry's second pitch deep to left. Home run. Jubilant fans circled the bases with Maz, celebrating another remarkable World Series triumph by the Pirates.

Pittsburgh has always had a rich tradition of slugging. The Pirates have won 20 league batting titles, including eight by Honus Wagner, four by Roberto Clemente, and three by Paul Waner. Ralph Kiner won or shared the National League home-run crown seven times and Willie Stargell won it twice.

Wagner, a .329 lifetime hitter, led Pittsburgh to pennants in 1901, 1902, and 1903, the year the Bucs lost the first-ever World Series, to the Boston Red Sox.

They won their first World Series in 1909,

● *Followed by a jubilant fan, Bill Mazeroski nears home plate after hitting the homer that won the 1960 World Series over the Yankees.*

against the Detroit Tigers, and did it again in 1925, against the Washington Senators. Two years later they were swept by the Yankees.

It took 33 years before they got into another World Series, but in between there were some glorious moments, including a game Harvey Haddix pitched in Milwaukee on May 26, 1959. He threw 12 perfect innings before losing to the Braves, 1–0, in the thirteenth.

It was a year later that the Pirates, with such stars as Bob Friend, Vernon Law, Dick Groat, Clemente, and, of course, Mazeroski, downed the Yankees in the World Series.

With Clemente batting .341 during the season and .414 in the Series, and Willie Stargell winning the homer (48) and RBI (154) titles, the Bucs won another World Series, in seven games, over Baltimore in 1971.

The baseball world mourned on December 31, 1972, when, at age 38, Clemente died in a plane crash on a mercy mission to earthquake-ravaged Nicaragua.

The Pirates, maintaining their streak in post-season play, were led by Willie Stargell in 1979 when they bounced back from trailing three-to-one in games to defeat Baltimore in the World Series.

PIVOT.   The pitcher's pivot foot is the foot that is in contact with the pitcher's plate as he delivers the pitch.

PLATOON.   The practice of using two different men for one position, common in football and frequently used in baseball. The greatest believer in platoon baseball was Casey Stengel, who often had one team to play against right-handed pitchers, another against left-handed pitchers. Although the law of averages supports the idea that a left-handed hitter does better against a right-handed pitcher and a right-handed

hitter does better against a left-handed pitcher, players like Babe Ruth, Joe DiMaggio, Hank Aaron, Stan Musial, Willie Mays, Rod Carew, and George Brett never had to be platooned.

PLAYER REPRESENTATIVE. *See* Major League Baseball Players Association.

PLAYOFF.   Since 1969 this term has taken on a new meaning. It is a series of games between champions of the Eastern and Western divisions in both leagues. The winner of the playoff is declared the pennant winner and represents its league in the World Series.

While baseball officially refers to this best-of-five series as the National (or American) League Championship Series, it is more popularly known as the National (or American) League Playoff.

Originally a playoff meant an unscheduled series of games that was required when two (or more) teams were tied in games at the end of the regular season. The playoff was necessary to determine the pennant winner.

For the first 45 years of this century, there were no major-league playoffs, although there were five in the next 20 years.

In 1946 the Brooklyn Dodgers and the St. Louis Cardinals finished the season tied for first place in the National League. It was decided that they would play a series of three games, the winner of two of them to be crowned champion. The Cardinals defeated the Dodgers in the first two games, making a third game unnecessary.

The American League got into the act two years later when the Boston Red Sox tied the Cleveland Indians. They decided to play just one game to decide the winner. Cleveland defeated Boston and earned the right to represent the American League in the World Series.

• *Celebrating the New York Giants' playoff victory over the Brooklyn Dodgers for the 1951 pennant (left to right): Bobby Thomson, winning pitcher Larry Jansen, and starter Sal Maglie*

All the National League's first four playoffs involved the Dodgers. In Brooklyn they lost to St. Louis in 1946 and to the New York Giants in 1951. In Los Angeles they beat the Milwaukee Braves in 1959 and lost to the San Francisco Giants in 1962.

The most memorable of all playoffs, however, was the one involving the Brooklyn Dodgers and the New York Giants in 1951. Behind by 13½ games as late as August, the Giants stormed back to tie the Dodgers in the last days of the season. The Giants won the first playoff game and the Dodgers the second, setting up the third game as "sudden death."

Going into the last of the ninth inning, the Dodgers led, 4–1. The Giants began hitting Don Newcombe, the starting Dodger pitcher. A series of hits made the score 4–2, and the Giants had two runners on base with just one out. Dodger manager Charlie Dressen replaced Newcombe with Ralph Branca, and Giant Bobby Thomson hit Branca's second pitch for the most dramatic home run in baseball history. The Giants

won the game, 5–4, and the right to play in the World Series, climaxing what has been romantically described as the Little Miracle of Coogan's Bluff (Coogan's Bluff overlooked the Polo Grounds, where the game was played).

Since the Championship Series format began in 1969, a single-game playoff has been held to break first-place ties. In 1978 the New York Yankees defeated the Boston Red Sox on a three-run homer by Bucky Dent, and in 1980 the Houston Astros won over the Los Angeles Dodgers.

POP FLY. A ball hit on a high fly to the infield, which is usually easily caught. Also called a pop-up and, when in foul territory, a foul pop.

PRESS BOX. The quarters assigned to reporters at the game, usually equipped with communication facilities. It is the place from which reporters view the game and write the stories that appear in the next day's newspapers. Press boxes have evolved from the old wooden boxes (still used in some minor-league parks) to modern, plush quarters.

PROMOTER.

In its early years baseball got so much free publicity that all the owners had to do was to open the gates and the people would come. But when other professional sports and television began to compete for the entertainment dollar, many club owners realized they had to advertise their product, although a number clung to the old notion that baseball did not need promoting.

The most flamboyant and most successful promoter in the game was Bill Veeck, who owned, at different times, the St. Louis Browns, Cleveland Indians, and Chicago White Sox and, not accidentally, set attendance records with each of them. Veeck used

● *Three-foot, seven-inch Eddie Gaedel pinch-hit for the St. Louis Browns against the Detroit Tigers in 1951—a stunt conceived by promoter-owner Bill Veeck.*

circus-type promotional stunts with unprecedented success. He gave away orchids to ladies and established a baby-sitting room so that young parents could go to the ballpark and not have to worry about what to do with their kids. His stunts were endless. His most famous one was using a midget, Eddie Gaedel, as a pinch-hitter in a regulation ball game.

Baseball's sideshows, as promoted by Veeck and others like him, are most common in the minor leagues and may feature anything from golf exhibitions to weddings at home plate. They may include fireworks, songfests, clown acts, foot races, beauty parades, giveaway shows, and participation by the players in such events as hitting baseballs into the stands, throwing a ball into a barrel, heaving raw eggs at each other, and milking a cow.

Veeck was scorned by his competitors, but many of his innovations, including an exploding scoreboard, are still used. Today most major-league clubs have Old-Timers' Day, Bat Day, Banner Day, and Camera Day, which are nothing more than promotional gimmicks.

● *Cow-milking contests have long been a sideshow in the minor leagues and occasionally in the big leagues.*

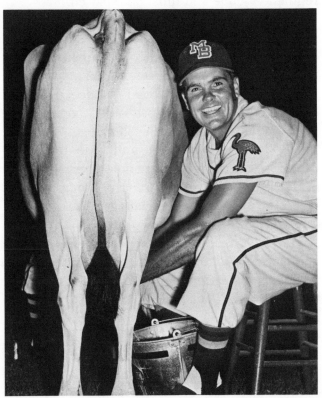

PULL HITTER. One who consistently and effectively hits a ball down or close to the foul line—left field for a right-handed hitter, right field for a left-handed hitter. It is so called because the action of a right-handed hitter leaves him pointing in the direction of left field when he has followed through. If a right-handed hitter hits to right field or a left-handed hitter to left field, it is called hitting to the opposite field or pushing the ball, a very useful device if done successfully. One who can hit the ball well to all fields is called a spray hitter.

PUTOUT. The retiring of an opponent by a defensive player.

QUICK PITCH. Also, a quick return. A pitch thrown hurriedly with the obvious intention of catching the batter unprepared. If it is detected by the umpire—which happens rarely—a quick pitch is called a balk, entitling all runners to advance one base. If the bases are empty, it is called a ball.

RAINCHECK. Ticket stub good for future admission if less than 4½ innings have been played before the game is called.

Rainchecks were first used in New Orleans in 1888. The word has been taken into general slang and means to turn down an invitation while expressing the hope that it will be good at a later date.

RECORDS. Baseball, more than any other sport, has hundreds of all-time records, covering every position and every category imaginable. As Casey Stengel, the most famous baseball manager of all, used to say: "You can look it up."

The records on the next two pages are the major ones, for batting and pitching. (*See also* Statistician.)

REGULATION GAME. A game that has come to a decision after the prescribed nine innings or more. Also, a game that has been called off, for whatever reason, after the losing team has been to bat five times. If it is called off before that time or if it is tied when it is called off, it is not a regulation game and must be replayed.

RELIEF PITCHER. A substitute pitcher who replaces the starting pitcher or another relief pitcher. Relief pitchers fall into three basic categories—the mop-up man, the long man, and the short man.

The mop-up man is usually the man considered to be the weakest or least experienced pitcher on the team. He comes in when the outcome of the game is no longer in doubt.

The long man is usually an alternate starter who gets the call when the starting pitcher gets in trouble early in the game, within the first four innings. The long man is expected to pitch anywhere from five to seven good innings.

The short man is the famed fireman, the relief specialist whom no good team can do without. He comes in late in the game when the score is close and the situation is serious

Batting

CAREER

Games Played	3,298	Hank Aaron, Milwaukee-Atlanta (NL), Milwaukee (AL), 1954–1976
Batting Average	.367	Ty Cobb, Detroit (AL), Philadelphia (AL), 1905–1928
At-Bats	12,364	Hank Aaron, Milwaukee-Atlanta (NL), Milwaukee (AL), 1954–1976
Runs Scored	2,245	Ty Cobb, Detroit (AL), Philadelphia (AL), 1905–1928
Hits	4,190	Ty Cobb, Detroit (AL), Philadelphia (AL), 1905–1928
Doubles	793	Tris Speaker, Boston-Cleveland-Washington-Philadelphia (all AL), 1907–1928
Triples	312	Sam Crawford, Cincinnati (NL), Detroit (AL), 1899–1917
Home Runs	755	Hank Aaron, Milwaukee-Atlanta (NL), Milwaukee (AL), 1954–1976
Runs Batted In	2,297	Hank Aaron, Milwaukee-Atlanta (NL), Milwaukee (AL), 1954–1976
Stolen Bases	938	Lou Brock, Chicago (NL), St. Louis (NL), 1961–1979
Bases on Balls	2,056	Babe Ruth, Boston (AL), New York (AL), Boston (NL), 1914–1935
Strikeouts	1,903	Willie Stargell, Pittsburgh (NL), 1962–1981

SEASON

Games Played	165	Maury Wills, Los Angeles (NL), 1962
Batting Average	.438	Hugh Duffy, Boston (NL), 1894
At-Bats	705	Willie Wilson, Kansas City (AL), 1980
Runs Scored	196	William Hamilton, Philadelphia (NL), 1894
Hits	257	George Sisler, St. Louis (AL), 1920
Doubles	67	Earl Webb, Boston (AL), 1931
Triples	36	J. Owen Wilson, Pittsburgh (NL), 1912
Home Runs	61	Roger Maris, New York (AL), 1961 (162-game schedule)
	60	Babe Ruth, New York (AL), 1927 (154-game schedule)
Runs Batted In	190	Hack Wilson, Chicago (NL), 1930
Stolen Bases	118	Lou Brock, St. Louis (NL), 1974
Bases on Balls	170	Babe Ruth, New York (AL), 1923
Strikeouts	189	Bobby Bonds, San Francisco (NL), 1970

GAME

At-Bats	11	Ten players; last done by Dave Cash, Montreal (NL), May 21, 1977 (21 innings)
Runs	6	Eleven players; last done by Frank Torre, Milwaukee (NL), September 2, 1957 (first game)
Hits	9	John Burnett, Cleveland (AL), July 10, 1932 (18 innings)
Doubles	4	Thirty-one players; last done by Dave Duncan, Baltimore (AL), June 30, 1975 (second game)
Triples	4	William Joyce, New York (NL), May 18, 1897
Home Runs	4	Ten players; last done by Mike Schmidt, Philadelphia (NL), April 17, 1976 (10 innings)
Runs Batted In	12	Jim Bottomley, St. Louis (NL), September 16, 1924
Stolen Bases	7	George Gore, Chicago (NL), June 25, 1881; William Hamilton, Philadelphia (NL), August 31, 1894 (second game)
Bases on Balls	6	Walter Wilmot, Chicago (NL), August 22, 1891; Jimmie Foxx, Boston (AL), June 16, 1938
Strikeouts	6	Five players; last done by Cecil Cooper, Boston (AL), June 14, 1974 (15 innings)

Pitching

CAREER

Games	1,070	Hoyt Wilhelm, New York (NL), St. Louis (NL), Cleveland (AL), Baltimore (AL), Chicago (AL), California (AL), Atlanta (NL). Chicago (NL), Los Angeles (NL), 1952–1972
Innings	7,377	Cy Young, Cleveland (NL), St. Louis (NL), Boston (AL), Cleveland (AL), Boston (NL), 1890–1911
Victories	511	Cy Young, Cleveland (NL), St. Louis (NL), Boston (AL), Cleveland (AL), Boston (NL), 1890–1911
Losses	313	Cy Young, Cleveland (NL), St. Louis (NL), Boston (AL), Cleveland (AL), Boston (NL), 1890–1911
Saves	244	Rollie Fingers, Oakland (AL), St. Louis (NL), Milwaukee (AL), 1968–1981
Strikeouts	3,508	Walter Johnson, Washington (AL), 1907–1927
Bases on Balls	1,778	Nolan Ryan, New York (NL), California (AL), Houston (NL), 1966–1981
Earned-Run Average (3,000 or more innings)	2.37	Walter Johnson, Washington (AL), 1907–1927
Shutouts	110	Walter Johnson, Washington (AL), 1907–1927

SEASON

Games	106	Mike Marshall, Los Angeles (NL), 1974
Innings	683	William White, Cincinnati (NL), 1879
Innings (since 1900)	464	Edward Walsh, Chicago (AL), 1908
Victories	60	Charles Radbourn, Providence (NL), 1884
Victories (since 1900)	41	Jack Chesbro, New York (AL), 1904
Losses	48	John Coleman, Philadelphia (NL), 1883
Losses (since 1900)	29	Victor Willis, Boston (NL), 1905
Saves	38	John Hiller, Detroit (AL), 1973
Strikeouts	411	Charles Radbourn, Providence (NL), 1884
Strikeouts (since 1900)	383	Nolan Ryan, California (AL), 1973
Bases on Balls	276	Amos Rusie, New York (NL), 1890
Earned-Run Average (300 or more innings)	1.12	Bob Gibson, St. Louis (NL), 1968
Shutouts	16	George Bradley, St. Louis (NL), 1876; Grover Cleveland Alexander, Philadelphia (NL), 1916

GAME

Innings Pitched	26	Leon Cadore, Brooklyn (NL); Joseph Oeschger, Boston (NL), May 1, 1920
Runs	35	David Rowe, Cleveland (NL), July 24, 1882
Runs (since 1900)	24	Aloysius Travers, Detroit, May 19, 1912
Hits	36	John Wadsworth, Louisville (NL), August 17, 1894
Hits (since 1900)	26	Harley Parker, Cincinnati (NL), June 21, 1901; Horace Lisenbee, Philadelphia (AL), September 11, 1936
Strikeouts	21	Thomas Cheney, Washington (AL), September 12, 1962 (16 innings)
Strikeouts (9-inning game)	19	Four players; last done by Nolan Ryan, California (AL), August 12, 1974
Bases on balls	16	Three players; last done by Bruno Haas, Philadelphia (AL), June 23, 1915

● *Hugh Casey saved many a Dodger starter as a fireman in the late 1940s.*

but not hopeless. He is the fireman because he is called in to put out the fire (an opposing team's rally).

The fireman is a vital member of the team, and he has gained great prominence in recent years, although his importance was acknowledged as far back as the mid-1920s, when Wilcy Moore and Firpo Marberry were the first of the great firemen. Marberry appeared in 64 games for the Washington Senators in 1926 and was so important to the team that they would delay the starting time so that when Firpo was ready to go to work, late in the game, shadows would have begun to descend and his fastball would be more effective.

Johnny Murphy of the New York Yankees was the leading fireman in the 1930s, but it wasn't until the early 1940s that Hugh Casey of the Brooklyn Dodgers and Joe Page of the Yankees began to get proper recognition for the rescue squad. Ace Adams appeared in 70 games for the New York Giants in 1943, and Jim Konstanty topped that for the Philadelphia Phillies in 1950, appearing in 74 games and winning the National League Most Valuable Player Award, a first for a relief pitcher. Konstanty's record was

broken by Mike Marshall of the Los Angeles Dodgers, who pitched in 106 games in 1974.

Among the top modern firemen are Bruce Sutter, Rich Gossage, Rollie Fingers, and Tug McGraw.

RESERVE CLAUSE. The controversial clause binding a player to his team. It was an important part of baseball for more than 50 years until it was buried by agreement in the summer of 1976. The standard players' contract had said that a player signing for one year also agreed to play for the club the year after, if the club wanted him to. Since players always signed contracts each year before being permitted to play, the reserve clause was, in effect, a contract for life.

Under the historic 1976 agreement, unsigned players in the 1976 season had the right to become free agents at the end of that season; signed players could become free agents after playing out the renewal year in their current contracts; and in future contracts a player with six years' major-league service has the right to ask to be traded at the end of a season, and he may list a maximum of six clubs to which he doesn't want to be traded. If he isn't traded by the following March 15, he becomes a free agent. (*See also* Draft.)

● *Rich Gossage of the Yanks rates as one of the best relief pitchers.*

RESIN BAG. A bag that is placed in back of the pitcher's mound and from which he may rub resin, a sticky substance, on his hands in order to dry them, though he may not rub resin on the ball. Resin is the only thing the pitcher may rub on his hand, but that does not stop pitchers from trying (and succeeding in some cases) to use such sticky substances as hair tonic, saliva, and petroleum jelly. The purpose of resin is to keep the ball from slipping. It is also used at certain times by a batter when his hands perspire so much that gripping the bat is difficult. In recent years batters have switched from resin to a rag saturated with pine tar, another sticky substance.

RHUBARB. A baseball controversy or argument, particularly an explosive one, on the field. Red Barber, who was a distinguished broadcaster with the Cincinnati Reds, Brooklyn Dodgers, and New York Yankees, began using the expression on the air in 1939 after picking it up from baseball writers Garry Schumacher and Tom Meany, who in turn heard the word used by a Brooklyn bartender to describe a barroom brawl. A variation, also used by Barber, was, "They're tearing up the pea patch."

• *Billy Martin could always be counted on to inspire a rhubarb whether he was with the Yankees or any other team.*

RIBBY. Players' slang for runs batted in, derived from trying to pronounce its initials: RBI.

RIGHT FIELD. The outfield territory beyond first base bordered on the right by the right foul line and on the left by the area covered by the center fielder. The outfielder who covers right field is called the right fielder.

ROBINSON, FRANK. It was on October 3, 1974, that Frank Robinson was named major-league baseball's first black manager. His job with the Cleveland Indians lasted less than three seasons, but he got another chance when he took over as manager of the San Francisco Giants in 1981.

As a player, Robinson proved himself time and again. He is the only one to win the Most Valuable Player Award in both leagues —with the Cincinnati Reds in 1961 and the Baltimore Orioles in 1966, when he won the Triple Crown (the league leader in batting average, RBI's, and home runs). He also played with the Los Angeles Dodgers, the California Angels, and the Cleveland Indians for a total of 21 seasons in which he hit 586 home runs and posted a lifetime batting average of .294.

An all-star outfielder, Robinson was born in Beaumont, Texas, on August 31, 1935, the youngest of 10 children.

ROBINSON, JACKIE. The abuse poured down on him, from the stands where fans cupped their hands around their mouths and shouted racial insults, and from the dugouts, where opposing players did the same thing. On the field Jackie Robinson, the first black man in organized baseball and the first of his race to make it to the major leagues, stood with his hands on his hips, trying not to show his emotions as his blood boiled inside.

After a few moments Robinson felt an arm around his shoulders. There beside him stood Pee Wee Reese, a native of Kentucky and captain of the Brooklyn Dodgers in that summer of 1947. Reese's gesture was symbolic, an eloquent statement of support for a man facing the greatest pressure and test of character imaginable.

Robinson had been carefully selected by Dodger owner Branch Rickey as the man who would shatter baseball's color line. "I'm looking for a ballplayer with guts enough *not* to fight back," Rickey told Robinson. To his credit Robinson, one of the game's fiercest competitors, kept his pledge to Rickey and turned the other cheek to the abuse being heaped on him. His courage forced open the doors of the sport to blacks, who had been previously barred from the majors.

Robinson was born in Cairo, Georgia, on January 31, 1919, and was a four-sport college star at UCLA. Rickey plucked him out of baseball's black leagues in 1946 and changed the face of baseball forever.

In 10 seasons with the Brooklyn Dodgers,

● *Jackie Robinson, the first black in organized baseball, played for the Montreal Royals before joining the Brooklyn Dodgers.*

Robinson achieved a .311 batting average and hit over .300 six times. He played on six pennant winners and was the National League batting champion and MVP in 1949 when he batted .342. His base-path daring—taunting pitchers with fake starts—and clutch hitting made him the unquestioned leader of the Dodgers.

● *Jackie Robinson's running and sliding gave fits to the opposition.*

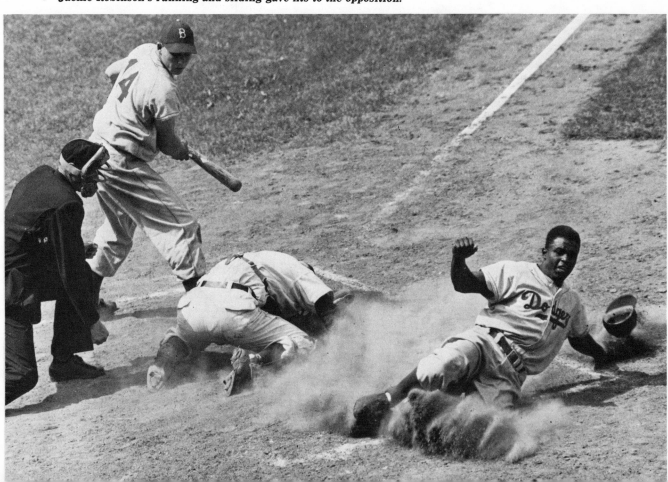

Robinson was elected to the Hall of Fame in 1962, his first year of eligibility. Ten years later, at age 53, he died of a heart attack.

ROOKIE. Also, a rook. A first-year player. Traditionally rookies are supposed to be innocent, and veteran players often take advantage of this by making them the butt of their inevitable gags. The most famous gag is to give the rookie a message to call a Mrs. Lyons. When the rookie calls the number given him, he finds he has reached the zoo.

Outstanding rookies are candidates for the Rookie-of-the-Year award given in each league. They are chosen by the Baseball Writers Association of America, whose votes are based on best all-around performance. The award was begun by the National League in 1947 and by the American League in 1949.

Rookie of the Year

NATIONAL LEAGUE

Year	Player, Club	Year	Player, Club
1947	Jackie Robinson, Brooklyn Dodgers	1965	Jim Lefebvre, Los Angeles Dodgers
1948	Al Dark, Boston Braves	1966	Tommy Helms, Cincinnati Reds
1949	Don Newcombe, Brooklyn Dodgers	1967	Tom Seaver, New York Mets
1950	Sam Jethroe, Boston Braves	1968	Johnny Bench, Cincinnati Reds
1951	Willie Mays, New York Giants	1969	Ted Sizemore, Los Angeles Dodgers
1952	Joe Black, Brooklyn Dodgers	1970	Carl Morton, Montreal Expos
1953	Junior Gilliam, Brooklyn Dodgers	1971	Earl Williams, Atlanta Braves
1954	Wally Moon, St. Louis Cardinals	1972	Jon Matlack, New York Mets
1955	Bill Virdon, St. Louis Cardinals	1973	Gary Matthews, San Francisco Giants
1956	Frank Robinson, Cincinnati Reds	1974	Bake McBride, St. Louis Cardinals
1957	Jack Sanford, Philadelphia Phillies	1975	John Montefusco, San Francisco Giants
1958	Orlando Cepeda, San Francisco Giants	1976	Pat Zachry, Cincinnati Reds
1959	Willie McCovey, San Francisco Giants		Butch Metzger, San Diego Padres
1960	Frank Howard, Los Angeles Dodgers	1977	Andre Dawson, Montreal Expos
1961	Billy Williams, Chicago Cubs	1978	Bob Horner, Atlanta Braves
1962	Kenny Hubbs, Chicago Cubs	1979	Rick Sutcliffe, Los Angeles Dodgers
1963	Pete Rose, Cincinnati Reds	1980	Steve Howe, Los Angeles Dodgers
1964	Richie Allen, Philadelphia Phillies	1981	Fernando Valenzuela, Los Angeles Dodgers

AMERICAN LEAGUE

Year	Player, Club	Year	Player, Club
1949	Roy Sievers, St. Louis Browns	1966	Tommie Agee, Chicago White Sox
1950	Walt Dropo, Boston Red Sox	1967	Rod Carew, Minnesota Twins
1951	Gil McDougald, New York Yankees	1968	Stan Bahnsen, New York Yankees
1952	Harry Byrd, Philadelphia Athletics	1969	Lou Piniella, Kansas City Royals
1953	Harvey Kuenn, Detroit Tigers	1970	Thurman Munson, New York Yankees
1954	Bob Grim, New York Yankees	1971	Chris Chambliss, Cleveland Indians
1955	Herb Score, Cleveland Indians	1972	Carlton Fisk, Boston Red Sox
1956	Luis Aparicio, Chicago White Sox	1973	Al Bumbry, Baltimore Orioles
1957	Tony Kubek, New York Yankees	1974	Mike Hargrove, Texas Rangers
1958	Albie Pearson, Washington Senators	1975	Fred Lynn, Boston Red Sox
1959	Bob Allison, Washington Senators	1976	Mark Fidrych, Detroit Tigers
1960	Ron Hansen, Baltimore Orioles	1977	Eddie Murray, Baltimore Orioles
1961	Don Schwall, Boston Red Sox	1978	Lou Whitaker, Detroit Tigers
1962	Tom Tresh, New York Yankees	1979	John Castino, Minnesota Twins
1963	Gary Peters, Chicago White Sox		Alfredo Griffin, Toronto Blue Jays
1964	Tony Oliva, Minnesota Twins	1980	Joe Charboneau, Cleveland Indians
1965	Curt Blefary, Baltimore Orioles	1981	Dave Righetti, New York Yankees

• *Pete Rose keeps a watchful eye on a promising prospect, Pete Jr., at a workout in Philadelphia's Veterans Stadium before the 1980 World Series.*

ROSE, PETE. The ball popped into the air, a simple foul ball, an easy play. For a moment the tension of the ninth inning in the deciding game of the 1980 World Series relaxed. Bob Boone, the sure-handed Philadelphia catcher, settled easily under the ball.

Then Boone stumbled and thrust out his glove, and the ball popped in and out as the Phillie fans gasped. But in a second Pete Rose, the first baseman, saved the out by grabbing the ball before it fell to the ground. The man they call Charlie Hustle had struck again.

"No big deal," explained Rose. "That's where I was supposed to be." But it *was* a big deal because that catch with the bases loaded moved the Phillies to within one out of the first world championship in the team's history.

It was a world championship that Rose helped deliver with his enthusiastic, gung-

ho style of play. Hall of Famer Whitey Ford had pinpointed it 17 years earlier when Rose, then a Cincinnati rookie, ran to first base after drawing a walk in a spring-training game. "Hey, Charlie Hustle, take it easy," teased Ford. Rose hasn't taken it easy yet.

Born on April 4, 1941, in Cincinnati, Rose was a hometown hero for 16 seasons with the Reds, establishing a number of club records. He left as a free agent, and the Phillies, figuring his aggressive style was just what the club needed to become a winner, signed him in 1979, one year after he set a modern National League record by hitting in 44 straight games.

Rose came to the majors as a second baseman and later switched to left field, third base, and first base, mastering each position to help the needs of his team. He was Rookie of the Year in 1963, Most Valuable Player in 1973, and World Series MVP in 1975. Ten times he has had 200-hit seasons —a major-league record—and in 1981, at the age of 40, he broke Stan Musial's record (3,631) for the most hits in the National League.

RUBBER. The pitcher's plate.

RUBBER ARM. A pitcher who can work day after day and maintain effectiveness. Such a pitcher was Mike Marshall, a relief pitcher for the Los Angeles Dodgers, who set a major-league record by appearing in 106 of his team's 162 games in 1974.

In baseball history there have been 39 pitchers who have pitched and won two complete games in one day, the last being Emil Levsen of the Cleveland Indians in 1926. Four men performed that rubber-arm stunt twice, and another, Joe McGinnity of the New York Giants, did it three times in one month, earning him the nickname Iron Man.

RUBBER GAME. The deciding or odd game of a series that will break a tie in that series is called the rubber game.

RUN. The score made by an offensive player who advances from the batter's box and touches first, second, third, and home in that order. "Let's get some runs" is probably the most widely used and oft-repeated phrase in baseball.

The modern major-league record for most runs in a game is 49, made when the Chicago White Sox defeated the Philadelphia Athletics, 26–23, on August 25, 1922. The Boston Red Sox and the White Sox share the modern record for most runs by a team in a game at 29. The Red Sox made theirs against the St. Louis Browns on June 8, 1950; the White Sox against the Kansas City A's on April 23, 1955. In 1953 the Red Sox set a modern record by scoring 17 runs in a single inning.

RUNDOWN. The defensive act that attempts to put out a runner caught between bases.

RUNS BATTED IN. Also known as RBI's, or ribbies. Credit given to a batter for each run that scores when he makes a safe hit, is retired by an infield or outfield putout, or when a run is forced in because he becomes a base runner. This is the lifeblood of the offense and the most coveted statistic by hitters, even more than hits, homers, or batting average.

All-time home-run champ Hank Aaron has the most career RBI's, 2,297. Babe Ruth shares with Lou Gehrig and Jimmie Foxx the record for having 13 years of 100 or more RBI's each year, although Hack Wilson of the Chicago Cubs holds the record for the most RBI's in a single season, 190 in 1930.

The following year Lou Gehrig set the American League record of 184. Jim Bottomley of the St. Louis Cardinals had 12 RBI's in one game in 1924, and seven players in modern times have knocked in six runs in an inning, including Sam Mele of the Chicago White Sox in 1952, and Jim Ray Hart of the San Francisco Giants in 1970.

RUTH, BABE. The bat sat back on Babe Ruth's shoulder as the pitcher began his windup. As the delivery was made, Ruth cocked the bat, dipping it in time with the pitch. Then he swung.

When he connected just right, the crack of the bat, wood smashing ball, commanded attention. The ball soared toward right field, and Ruth, the master of the dramatic, would watch it as it sailed for the seats. Then the Babe would break into his home-run trot, mincing steps on bandy legs that seemed strained to the limit carrying his top-heavy body.

The Babe was an American hero, a legendary character who sometimes seemed larger than life. In the 1920s, the Golden Age of Sports, no man dominated the scene as completely as Ruth. He had a gusto that captivated everyone.

Ruth, of course, was the greatest home-run hitter of his time, setting a career record of 714 and a single-season mark of 60 (in 1927). Both records were eventually broken but they remain cherished numbers in baseball lore.

When Yankee Stadium was built in 1923, its inviting short right field was perfect for the left-handed Ruth. The Babe flourished there and hit the first home run in the stadium's history. He also hit the first All-Star Game homer in 1933.

Ruth hit 50 or more homers in a season four times and led his league in runs batted in six times. He finished his career with a .342 batting average.

The Babe was born in Baltimore on Feb-

● *Before he became an outfielder, Babe Ruth was an outstanding pitcher with the Boston Red Sox.*

ruary 6, 1895, and came to the majors in 1914 as a pitcher with the Boston Red Sox. In 1916 he posted a 23-12 record and led the league with a 1.75 earned-run average. A year later he won 24 games and posted a 2.01 ERA. He set a record of 29⅔ scoreless innings in a row in the World Series and posted a 3-0 record and 0.87 ERA in the Series that year.

But Ruth was too good a hitter to remain a pitcher, which he proved after being sold to the Yankees. He was a charter member of the Hall of Fame and was mourned by millions when he died in 1948 at age 53.

RYAN, NOLAN. Cesar Geronimo stepped into the batter's box, and on the mound Nolan Ryan swung into his windup. Ryan kicked his left leg into the air, cocked his right arm, and brought his body forward. His leg came down, and he planted his foot firmly as his arm came forward. The effect was like a slingshot—the baseball hurtled toward the plate at about 100 miles per hour.

Geronimo was overmatched and the home-plate umpire's right arm shot into the air. "Strike three!" he shouted, and with that one pitch the slender Houston Astro pitcher with the exploding fastball moved into the record books. It was his three-thousandth strikeout, making him a member of an exclusive club. When Ryan reached that magic 3,000 mark, the only other pitchers in baseball history to have accomplished the feat were Walter Johnson, Bob Gibson, and Gaylord Perry. Johnson and Gibson are in the Hall of Fame and Perry seems certain to join them. It's fast company for a fast pitcher.

Ryan may well have been baseball's fastest pitcher. He has been clocked at better than 100 mph and his speed has often made him simply unhittable. Going into 1982 he had pitched five no-hitters for the all-time record. Four of his no-hitters were pitched

for the California Angels, the first two just two months apart: on May 15, 1973, against Kansas City, and on July 15, 1973, against Detroit. He also no-hit Minnesota on September 28, 1974, Baltimore on June 1, 1975, and Los Angeles on September 26, 1981, the last as a member of the Astros.

Ryan, who was born on January 31, 1947, in Refugio, Texas, also has had seven one-hitters and holds the record for 15-strikeout games, achieving that feat a remarkable 21 times. He had five 300-strikeout seasons including a record 383 in 1973, his double no-hit season.

● *Nolan Ryan has struck out more than 3,000 batters.*

Geronimo, who was the victim when Ryan reached number 3,000 on July 4, 1980, earned a unique niche in baseball history with that strikeout. He also happened to be Gibson's three-thousandth strikeout victim a few years earlier.

SACRIFICE.

A play in which the batter is out but is not charged with an official time at bat because he has succeeded in moving a teammate along on the bases at the expense of his turn at bat, whether intentionally or not. There are two types of sacrifices: the sacrifice bunt (sometimes called a sacrifice hit) and the sacrifice fly.

The sacrifice bunt is hit, usually under orders, to advance another runner. The batter deliberately gives up his time at bat to improve his team's chances of scoring. The sacrifice fly is rarely done intentionally. It occurs only when a batter has hit a ball far enough so that a runner may score from third base after the catch. The batter gets an RBI and is credited with a sacrifice (no official time at bat) only if the runner scores.

SAFE.

A declaration by the umpire that a runner reached the base for which he was trying before the ball did. The umpire signals a runner safe by putting his hands down, palms parallel to the ground.

SAILER.

A pitched ball that takes off —that is, it sails upward as it approaches the batter.

ST. LOUIS CARDINALS.

The cat-and-mouse game was on. Philadelphia pitcher Dick Ruthven stepped off the rubber and fired to first. The Cards' Lou Brock scampered back ahead of the tag. As soon as Ruthven made his next pitch, Brock was off to the races.

It was, as it was so often with Brock, no contest. Sliding under Bob Boone's peg, Brock stole his 105th base of the 1974 season, breaking the record set by Los Angeles' Maury Wills in 1962. By the time he finished the 1974 season, Brock had swiped 118 bases. He retired in 1979 with a major-league career record of 938.

Aggressive base running—Enos Slaughter scored from first on a single for the winning run in the seventh game of the 1946 World Series against Boston—was just one of the ingredients that added up to 12 St. Louis pennants.

Only two years after winning his fifth straight batting crown with a modern record .424 average, Rogers Hornsby managed the Cards to the first of their dozen pennants.

In the 1926 World Series victory over the Yankees, pitcher Grover Cleveland Alexander had two wins and a save at the age of 39. Pepper Martin's 12 hits helped win the 1931 Series in seven games over Philadelphia. With Dizzy Dean becoming the last National League pitcher to win 30 games and with Ducky Medwick, player-manager Frankie Frisch, Leo Durocher, and Martin adding the fuel, the Cardinals' Gashouse Gang won a seven-game Series over the Tigers in

• *Pepper Martin, one of the St. Louis Cardinals' Gashouse Gang in the mid-1930s, demonstrates his sliding technique.*

1934. St. Louis was world champion again in 1942, 1944, and 1946.

Despite the presence of Stan (the Man) Musial, a .331 lifetime hitter, St. Louis didn't win another pennant until 1964, when Brock, Ken Boyer, Curt Flood, and Bob Gibson led the way to a seven-game triumph over the Yankees. And in 1967 they won the world championship again, over the Boston Red Sox.

Gibson, an overwhelming right-hander, fanned 17 Detroit players in the first game of the 1968 World Series against Detroit, but the Cardinals lost in seven. They haven't been in the winner's circle since that 1968 pennant.

SAN DIEGO PADRES. Nate Colbert was an eight-year-old sitting in St.

Louis' Busch Stadium in 1954 when Stan Musial slammed five homers in a doubleheader. "I never thought anyone would equal that record, certainly not me," said Colbert.

He was wrong. On August 1, 1972, in Atlanta, Colbert ripped five Braves' pitchers for five homers, including a grand slam, 13 RBI's, and seven runs scored. It stands as the most stunning hitting feat in the brief history of the Padres.

Colbert clouted 127 homers in his first four seasons with the club, and Dave Winfield came off the University of Minnesota campus to hit .277 as a rookie in 1973, but the Padres have always had a reputation as a light-hitting ballclub.

Named after the Pacific Coast League entry that brought Minnie Minoso, Al Rosen, and Ted Williams to San Diego during their minor-league careers, the Padres spent the years following their birth in 1969 wallowing in the second division.

Besides Winfield and Colbert, the team's most prominent names have been a pair of Cy Young Award winners—Randy Jones and Gaylord Perry. Jones won the honor in 1976 with a 22-14 season and a 2.74 ERA on the heels of a 20-12, 2.24-ERA season in

• *Randy Jones won the Cy Young Award as the National League's top pitcher in 1976.*

1975. Perry went 21-6 with a 2.72 ERA to win the award in 1978.

The most memorable near-achievement in club history belongs to Clay Kirby. He pitched eight innings of no-hit ball against the Mets in 1970, but was lifted for a pinch-hitter in the eighth with his team trailing, 1–0. The Padres lost the game and the relief pitcher blew the no-hitter.

On one occasion Ray Kroc, the team's owner, who made his fortune as the McDonald's hamburger king, was so disgusted by the play of his Padres that he seized the public address microphone and apologized for it. He offered everyone there a free admission in the future. Nobody knows how many fans took him up on his offer.

SANDLOT. An informal field, such as a vacant lot, meadow, or yard, on which youngsters play baseball. Before Little League just about every youngster in America played sandlot baseball. They were largely unorganized teams that rarely had uniforms and played on makeshift diamonds. In some places they were organized into teams, after a fashion, but most often a sandlot game would get started just as soon as a handful of boys had gathered.

SAN FRANCISCO GIANTS. It was known as "The Shot Heard 'Round the World." It happened in a playoff game in 1951, when New York Giant Bobby Thomson hit a ninth-inning home run off Brooklyn Dodger Ralph Branca to give the Giants a come-from-behind 5–4 victory and the National League pennant. Keyed by Rookie of the Year Willie Mays, the Giants had capped a comeback that saw them erase a 13½-game Dodger lead in the final six weeks.

In 1962 the Giants' playoff lightning struck the Dodgers again, but this time the Giants' home was in San Francisco and the Dodgers' was in Los Angeles. Trailing 4–2 in the ninth inning of the third game, the Giants rallied. Mays's bases-loaded single and Orlando Cepeda's sacrifice fly tied the game, and a walk forced in the winning run—as the Giants captured their eighteenth National League pennant.

The Giants' history dates back to the early 1900s. The club record book is dotted with Hall of Famers—John McGraw, Frankie Frisch, Bill Terry (the NL's last .400 hitter back in 1930), Carl Hubbell (253 wins), Christy Mathewson (373 wins), and Mel Ott (511 homers).

Their heated rivalry with the Dodgers did not lessen after the teams went west in 1958. The Giants added Willie (Stretch) McCovey (521 homers) and pitcher Juan Marichal (238 wins), and were constant contenders in the 1960s. Their last title came in 1971, when the 40-year-old Mays sparked them to a National League West crown.

● *High-kicking Juan Marichal won 238 games for the Giants.*

An era ended when the Giants traded Mays to the Mets in 1972—and the team has not been the same since.

SAVE. Credit given to a relief pitcher who finishes a game and protects a lead for another pitcher, who is credited with the victory. The rules grant a save to a pitcher who: 1. pitches at least three innings and protects a lead; or 2. enters the game with the potential tying run either on base or represented by one of the first two men he faces; or 3. enters with a lead of no more than three runs and pitches at least one inning.

SCHMIDT, MIKE. The standard had been established in 1953 when Mike Schmidt was four years old. That was the year that Eddie Mathews blasted 47 home runs, a record for third basemen.

Twenty-seven years later Schmidt stood at home plate in Montreal's Olympic Stadium. It was the next-to-last game of the 1980 National League season and the Eastern Division championship was at stake. Montreal and Philadelphia were locked in a head-to-head showdown. The teams had arrived at the final three games of the race in a tie for the lead.

Schmidt had driven in both runs in the opening game of the series and the Phillies won, 2–1. Now Philadelphia was one game away from the flag. But the Expos weren't surrendering quietly. The teams battled into the eleventh inning, tied at 4–4. Then Schmidt walloped a two-run homer, breaking the deadlock and delivering the deciding victory to the Phillies. It was his forty-eighth home run of the season, an all-time record for third basemen, one more than Eddie Mathews had managed 27 years before. And it gave Schmidt his fourth National League home-run title.

Schmidt, who was born on September 27,

● **Mike Schmidt was the World Series MVP when the Phillies won their first championship in 1980.**

1949, in Dayton, Ohio, went on to win MVP honors in the World Series as the Phillies captured the first world championship in the team's 98-year history. In 1980 he was the regular-season MVP as well, and in 1981 he repeated as National League home-run champ and MVP.

SCORECARD. A printed card that helps spectators identify the players, giving their numbers and positions, and on which an account of the game can be recorded. Scorecards are sold in the stands, and the familiar cry of the scorecard huckster is, "You can't tell the players without a scorecard."

Scorecards date back to the 1880s, when two young men named Harry Stevens and Ed Barrow sold scorecards in the ballpark at Wheeling, West Virginia, in the Tri-State League. Barrow went on to great success and Hall of Fame recognition as general manager of the New York Yankees. In 1890 Stevens went to New York to sell his score-cards and parlayed them into a multi-million-dollar concessions operation.

SCORING. The official scorer, usually a baseball writer, is appointed by the league president. With the job goes a welcome fee from the league and some unwelcome abuse from disgruntled athletes, up to and including an occasional punch in the nose. Apart from the official scorer, who is responsible for deciding on hits and errors and other rulings associated with the statistics of the game, all baseball writers and broadcasters and many fans keep score in books or on scorecards.

Scorekeeping methods vary, but there are a number of basics, including the system of giving each position a number. The standard numbering code is: 1. pitcher, 2. catcher, 3. first baseman, 4. second baseman, 5. third baseman, 6. shortstop, 7. left fielder, 8. center fielder, and 9. right fielder.

Fielding plays are recorded by number, with X often meaning a force play. Walks are B or W, strikeouts traditionally are K, or a backwards K (Я) for a called third strike. Base-path advances are noted by drawing the outline of a diamond, starting with home plate in the lower left corner or in the lower center and moving counterclockwise. A hit is usually a horizontal line (two lines for a double, three lines for a triple) crossed by a vertical or diagonal line to indicate the direction of the hit. A squiggly line indicates that a new pitcher has entered the game.

The accompanying score sheet is taken from the final game of the 1975 World Series, showing how the Cincinnati Reds beat the Boston Red Sox in the seventh game, 4–3.

Notice that in the first inning Pete Rose

started the game by flying out to the right fielder. Joe Morgan struck out swinging, and Johnny Bench grounded out, shortstop to first base.

In the third inning the Red Sox scored first, three runs, to take a 3–0 lead. After Bill Lee struck out swinging, Bernie Carbo walked. Denny Doyle and Carl Yastrzemski singled, Carbo scoring, and when the throw went home, Doyle went to third and Yastrzemski to second.

With first base open, Carlton Fisk was intentionally walked (IW). Fred Lynn struck out looking, but Rico Petrocelli walked to force in one run, and Dwight Evans walked to force in the third run before Rick Burleson struck out.

Cincinnati retaliated with two runs in the sixth on Rose's single and a home run by Tony Perez. They tied it in the seventh on a walk to Ken Griffey with one out, another walk to pinch-hitter Ed Armbrister with two out, and a single by Rose.

The final, and winning, run was scored in the top of the ninth. Griffey again walked and was sacrificed to second by Cesar Geronimo. Dan Driessen grounded out as a pinch-hitter, but Rose walked and Morgan singled to center to score Griffey with what proved to be the winning run.

In their final chance in the last of the ninth, the Red Sox went out in order. With Will McEnaney pitching for the Reds, Juan Beniquez batted for Rick Miller and flied to right. Bob Montgomery batted for Doyle and grounded to shortstop. Yastrzemski flied to center for the final out of the game, and the Cincinnati Reds were world champions!

SCOUT. Expert assigned to gather information on rival teams or, if he is a talent scout, to recruit players. A bird dog, usually a part-timer, sniffs out talent and gives leads to the scouts.

- *Scoring the seventh game of the 1975 World Series*

SCRATCH HIT. A batted ball that results in a base hit, although it is not solidly hit, usually just slipping away from an infielder as it dribbles past him.

SCREWBALL. The pitch (not the person) is a ball rolling in a reverse spin off the outer side of the middle finger. Its action is the opposite of a curveball, breaking away from a left-handed hitter and toward a right-handed hitter when thrown by a right-hander, and breaking away from a right-handed hitter and toward a left-handed hitter when thrown by a left-hander. Sometimes called a reverse curve, it was made popular by Carl Hubbell, the Giant left-hander, who used it when he struck out Babe Ruth, Lou Gehrig, Jimmie Foxx, Al Simmons, and Joe Cronin in a row in the 1934 All-Star Game. Players often call it the Scroogie.

● *Outfielder Ruppert Jones was one of the few Mariners the fans could cheer in Seattle.*

SEATTLE MARINERS. The 1977 season was a crucial one for baseball in Seattle. Thanks in part to the efforts of comedian Danny Kaye, one of the Mariner owners, Washington's largest city was being given a second chance at major-league baseball. In 1969 the Pilots had failed miserably in Seattle, and low attendance figures for their only season prompted a move to Milwaukee, where they became the Brewers in 1970.

This time around, however, the new Seattle franchise had an edge—a domed 59,000-seat stadium called the Kingdome, with not-very-distant fences. And the fans made sure it was filled most of the time that first season when 1,338,511 came out to watch the Mariners, nearly twice as many as had seen the Pilots in 1969.

The Mariners, the usual new-team collection of unprovens, unwanteds, and aging stars, got off to a fairly good start under former Boston manager Darrell Johnson, finishing with a 64-98 record and avoiding the basement in the American League West. But in 1978 they hit rock bottom.

Veteran slugger Willie Horton, in the twilight of an impressive career, and young outfielder Ruppert Jones, the only rookie to make the 1977 American League All-Star team, were among the few stars who managed to raise the team one position in 1979 over last-place Oakland. But by 1980 the

Mariners were last again, and Horton and Jones were gone.

Out of the rubble came one ray of hope. Late in the 1980 season Maury Wills, the former Los Angeles Dodger shortstop, became the manager. He seemed just the kind of leader the Mariners needed to make a move upward in the eighties. Unfortunately, Wills didn't have the magic or the players, and he was fired before he could finish 1981.

SEAVER, TOM. Tom Seaver stepped up on the mound and peered in for the sign from catcher Don Werner. The runner took a cautious lead off first base. Seaver glanced over, his mind racing. It was the ninth inning. Cincinnati was leading, 4–0, and St. Louis hadn't made a hit all game.

Seaver had been this route before. He had

• *Terrific Tom Seaver has achieved everything a pitcher could want—the Cy Young Award (three times), four 20-victory seasons, a world championship (with the Mets) and a no-hitter (with the Reds).*

pitched five one-hitters in his career. Three times he had carried no-hitters into the ninth inning only to have them broken up, once with two out and two strikes on the batter.

A no-hitter had been the one achievement to escape Seaver, the right-hander with the classic delivery who was one of baseball's finest pitchers during the seventies. He had won three Cy Young Awards and been a 20-game winner five times. He had come close, but he had never managed a pitcher's greatest achievement, a no-hitter. Now he was on the verge again.

"I couldn't really think too much about the no-hitter because I was concentrating on winning the game," Seaver said. "My philosophy has been, if it happens, it happens. If you pitch long enough, with good enough stuff, you are bound to pitch a no-hitter sooner or later."

So Seaver, unaffected by the pressure, proceeded to mow down the next three Cardinal batters in order—and did it at last. His no-hitter came on June 16, 1978—a year and a day after he had been traded to the Reds by the New York Mets.

Born on November 17, 1944, in Fresno, California, Seaver attended the University of Southern California, where he first attracted the attention of big-league scouts. When the Mets acquired his draft rights in 1965, it signaled the start of the Mets' development as a competitive club.

Seaver was Rookie of the Year in 1967. Among his many records, Seaver struck out 19 men in one game—including the last 10 in a row—in 1970, tying one major-league mark and setting another.

His career in New York ended bitterly with a contract dispute that led to his trade to the Reds early in the 1977 season.

SECOND BASE. The middle stop on the way around all four bases; the base a runner goes to after having reached first base. Second base, called the keystone, is in the middle of the diamond. The second baseman is responsible for the territory around and to the first-base side of second base.

SEMIPRO. One who receives money for playing, but does it outside of organized baseball and not as his sole source of income.

SENT TO THE SHOWERS. An expression meaning a pitcher was ineffective and had to be replaced. Often he is said to have gone for an early shower. During the summer of 1965 New York City had a drought, and city officials appealed to citizens to save water. One young citizen at Shea Stadium had his own idea about how New York could help fight the water shortage. He made his suggestion in the form of a banner that read: "Save Water—Don't Send Met Pitchers to the Showers."

SEVENTH-INNING STRETCH. The period during a game when fans customarily stand up, stretch, and show support for their team before it comes to bat in the seventh inning. Nobody knows how the tradition got started, not even veteran baseball writer Dan Daniel, the game's foremost historian. "It just grew, like Topsy," Dan said. "It probably originated as an expression of fatigue and tedium, which seems to explain why the stretch comes late in the game instead of at the halfway point."

SHAKE OFF. When a pitcher disagrees with the catcher's suggestion of which pitch should be thrown, he shakes off the catcher's signal with a prearranged signal of his own, usually by shaking his head or by flapping his glove back and forth.

SHOESTRING CATCH. To catch a line drive. This is usually done by an outfielder, who grabs the ball just as it is about to fall—or over his shoelaces, so to speak. It is one of the most difficult and, consequently, one of the most spectacular catches in the game.

SHORTSTOP. The infield position between second base and third base (sometimes called the short field); also, the infielder who covers this position.

SHUTOUT. When one team fails to score at all in the course of a game. Also called whitewash, calcimine, blank.

The record for shutouts in a career is 113, by Walter Johnson of the Washington Senators from 1907 to 1927. Grover Cleveland Alexander of the Philadelphia Phillies set the record for one season, 16 in 1916. And Don Drysdale pitched 58 shutout innings in a row in 1968—a record.

SIGNALS. When you see a third-base coach go through all kinds of gyrations, it does not necessarily mean he has ants in his pants. If he scratches his left ear, it may not be because he is itching; rather, he wants the man on first to try to steal second base on the next pitch. These are baseball signals used by the coach to tell the batters and runners what the manager wants them to do in a given situation, and by the catcher to suggest to the pitcher what pitch should be thrown.

Signals are usually intricate enough so the opposing team can't understand them and can't tell what's about to happen. Sometimes signals are so complicated that they are missed by the one for whom they are intended—which may result in a fine for the player who missed them. There is, however, no pattern to signals, and sometimes they are so simple they are difficult to detect.

Charlie Dressen was said to be the best at stealing the opposition's signals. There is a story about an All-Star Game when Charlie was sent to coach at third base.

"What signals are we using?" asked one player at a pregame meeting.

"Just use the signals you use with your regular team all season long," Charlie said. "I know them all."

The catcher signals before every pitch, and it is something of a baseball legend that the catcher's signals are one finger for a fastball and two for a curve. That is an oversimplification. The catcher actually works in a series. For example, he may arrange with the pitcher ahead of time that the real signal will be the second number he flashes. So he will flash four fingers, followed by two, two, three, one. Since the second signal is the one that counts, the pitcher knows the catcher wants a curveball because the second signal was two fingers.

The catcher can change the code every inning if he chooses; but he usually keeps the same code and becomes more cautious and his signals become more complex only when there is a runner on second base, from where it is easy to see the catcher's signals.

SINGLE. A base hit on which only first base is legally and safely reached. In 1927 Lloyd Waner got the incredible total of 198 one-base hits for the Pittsburgh Pirates, a modern-day record.

SINKER. Either a pitched or a batted ball that breaks downward.

SLICE. To hit a ball to the opposite field by accident. That is, a right-handed hitter hitting to right field and a left-handed hitter hitting to left field.

SLIDE. In order to make a smaller target for the fielder and to make sure not to overrun the base, a runner going into a base will often slide or "hit the dirt." Without breaking stride, he drops to the ground a few feet from the base. Some players slide on their bellies and go in head first, but the most common slide is feet first, with the player sliding on his side directly into the base. One of the prettiest and most exciting plays in baseball is the hook slide, in which the runner slides with his body flung away from the bag and hooks the bag with his trailing foot. This is done when the fielder has already received the ball and is waiting for the runner and a conventional slide would be useless.

SLUGGER. A powerful hitter. Usually the third, fourth, or fifth batter in the lineup.

SLUGGING PERCENTAGE. A method of determining a batter's effectiveness in making extra-base hits by dividing the batter's times at bat into his total bases and carrying the answer to three decimal places. For example, if a batter hits a home run (4 bases) in 4 at-bats, his slugging percentage would be 1.000. The maximum slugging percentage is 4.000, a home run every time at bat. In 1920 Babe Ruth had a remarkable slugging percentage of .847 on 388 total bases in 458 at-bats. For his career, Ruth had a slugging percentage of .692 on 5,762 total bases in 8,324 at-bats.

SLUMP. A long period of ineffectiveness, usually by a batter, but also by a team, a pitcher, or a fielder.

SNIDER, DUKE. Edwin Donald (Duke) Snider hasn't swung a bat for the Dodgers since 1962, but the 389 home runs

● *Home runs—more than 400—boomed Duke Snider into the Hall of Fame.*

and 1,271 RBI's he hit for them starting in 1947 still stand as club records.

Counting his last two years, when he played for the New York Mets and the San Francisco Giants, Duke rammed a total of 407 home runs. Duke is one of only two National League players to have hit 40 or more homers in five straight seasons. He played in six World Series, and he slammed four home runs in both the 1952 and 1955 Series.

Born in Los Angeles on September 19, 1926, Duke was a graceful center fielder who rivaled his New York counterparts, Yankee Mickey Mantle and Giant Willie Mays.

He was elected to the Hall of Fame in 1980.

SONGS. Baseball is America's favorite sport. Even songs have been written about it. The most popular is "Take Me Out to the Ball Game," which has long been baseball's theme song. It was written at the turn of the century by Jack Norworth and Albert Von Tilzer, and did as much for baseball as it did for its authors. Songs have been written about individual players—the most famous was "Joltin' Joe DiMaggio," which was a hit record just before World War II. Other songs have glorified Jackie Robinson, Willie Mays, and Mickey Mantle.

SPAHN, WARREN. The lanky pitcher swung into his windup, hands high over his head. As Warren Spahn brought his hands forward, he kicked his right leg high in the air. That kick was his trademark, the flourish at the end of the signature of one of the finest left-handers in baseball history.

No southpaw ever won more games than the 363 Spahn recorded in his 21-season National League career, all but one season with the Boston and later Milwaukee Braves.

He didn't win his first game until age 25, after three years of combat service in World War II. He made up for lost time fast, winning 20 or more games in 13 seasons over a 17-year period including six seasons in a row from 1956 to 1961. He pitched no-hitters in 1960 and 1961, the second one at age 40. In eight seasons he either led or tied for the lead in victories, and he was the National League earned-run-average leader three times.

Spahn, who was born in Buffalo, New York, on April 23, 1921, was not an overpowering pitcher, but he was a master of control, setting up hitters and nipping the corners of the plate.

Ironically, one of the few seasons in which Spahn failed to win 20 games was 1948, when he and Johnny Sain helped the

Boston Braves win the pennant. That was the year the fans coined the saying, "Spahn and Sain and pray for rain." That meant that if it rained when Spahn and Sain weren't scheduled to pitch, they'd have a chance to be rested and could take a turn on the mound ahead of their less-talented teammates.

SPIES. Every so often there is a rash of newspaper stories telling of teams being accused of planting spies in scoreboards or buildings in center field to steal the signals of the opposition catcher and pass them on to the batter by various prearranged signals. Usually the accusations are laughed at, denied, and then forgotten. However, the Chicago White Sox were exposed for spying not by the opposition but by one of their own players, Al Worthington, a pitcher of high principles who threatened to quit the team if the Sox did not stop spying. They stopped.

SPITBALL. A ball moistened on a small spot, either with saliva or perspiration, that sails or sinks in an unpredictable manner. For this reason the spitball (or spitter) is an illegal pitch. The spitball used to be a great weapon for the pitcher, but in 1920 baseball ruled against the spitball as well as the emery ball (roughing one side of the ball with emery paper), the talcum powder ball (one side of the ball was made slick by adding talcum powder), and the resin ball.

However, all those who were recognized spitball pitchers then in the major leagues were permitted to continue to use the pitch without penalty for the rest of their major-league careers. The last of the legal spitball pitchers was Burleigh Grimes, who pitched until 1934. Although the spitball has been illegal for half a century, it is generally believed that about 25 percent of modern major-league pitchers sometimes use it.

When Don Drysdale of the Los Angeles Dodgers was accused of throwing a spitball,

● *Warren Spahn pitched one of his two no-hitters when he was 40 years old.*

his only defense was, "My mother told me never to put my dirty fingers in my mouth."

Among the common expressions ballplayers use to say a pitcher threw a spitball are: "The bottom dropped out of that one," "That was a wet one," "He loaded that one up," or, to the umpire, "Give him a bucket."

SQUEEZE PLAY. A bunt with a man on third and less than two out. If the base runner starts for home as soon as the ball is being delivered, it is called a suicide squeeze. If he breaks for the plate after the ball has been bunted, it is a safety squeeze. In either case it is a difficult play, but a very effective weapon if properly done.

STARGELL, WILLIE. The ball jumped off Willie Stargell's bat, cutting through the night sky on a high arc—a rainbow shot labeled from the moment he hit it, bound for the Baltimore bullpen. It was to become a two-run homer, the deciding blow in the seventh game of the 1979 World Series, leading the Pittsburgh Pirates to the world championship.

It was entirely fitting for Stargell to strike the winning home run that season. Captain of the team, emotional leader of the Pirate family, he had spent the year distributing tiny gold stars to his teammates, saluting important contributions to the club's success. But no one contributed more than Stargell, who scored a stupendous sweep that year, sharing the regular-season MVP award with Keith Hernandez of the St. Louis Cardinals and then winning the playoff and Series awards by a wide margin.

Stargell was born on March 6, 1941, in Earlsboro, Oklahoma, and spent his entire big-league career with the Pirates. He holds two important batting records: four extra-base hits in a single game four times and 90 extra-base hits during the 1973 season. That was the year he led the league with 44 homers and 43 doubles.

• *Willie Stargell's blast won the 1979 World Series for the Pirates.*

But the year Stargell will remember best was 1979, when at the age of 38 he lifted his team to the championship.

STARTING PITCHER. The pitcher chosen to start the game. He is officially in the game once his name has been presented to the umpire-in-chief, and he must complete pitching to at least one batter unless he has suffered an injury that, in the judgment of the umpire, has been serious enough to sideline him.

STARTING ROTATION. The order in which a manager uses his starting pitchers, subject to change if one member of the rotation is in a slump. Ideally, most teams use a four-man rotation (each pitcher

137·

works every fourth game), but sometimes it becomes necessary to use a five-man rotation.

STATISTICIAN. A fellow who keeps records on the game. There are many amateur statisticians, including newspapermen and fans, but each team and both leagues employ official statisticians. The Elias Sports Bureau in New York is the official statistician for the National League; its counterpart for the American League is the Sports Information Center of North Quincy, Massachusetts. Both offer computerized daily baseball statistics.

Allan Roth revolutionized the use of statistics for ballclubs when he worked for the Dodgers in Brooklyn and Los Angeles. He recorded every pitch to every batter and kept massive records that were invaluable to the team. If the manager wanted to know how Joe Blow batted for a season with a count of no balls and two strikes against left-handed pitchers, for example, Roth could produce the answer almost immediately.

STEAL. A stolen base. It is credited to a runner who advances a base without benefit of a base hit, a fielder's choice, or an opponent's error. Speed is important, but good base stealers are also skilled at taking a lead, getting a jump on the pitch, and sliding. In 1915 Ty Cobb of the Detroit Tigers stole 96 bases, which stood as the record until Maury Wills of the Los Angeles Dodgers stole 104 in 1962. Then Lou Brock of the St. Louis Cardinals stole 118 bases in 1974. However, Cobb made his record in 156 games, Wills in 165 games, and Brock in 162 games.

STENGEL, CASEY. *See* Casey.

STENGELESE. A foreign language not taught by Berlitz. It was the unique double-talk of longtime manager Casey Stengel, who fractured the English language and charmed his audience in the process.

An example of Stengelese: "No manager is ever gonna run a tail-end club and be popular because there is no strikeout king that he's gonna go up and shake hands with and they're gonna love ya because who's gonna kiss a player when he strikes out and I got a shortstop which I don't think I coulda been a success without him if ya mix up the infield ya can't have teamwork and it's a strange thing if ya look it up that the Milwaukee club in the morning paper lost a doubleheader and they got three of my players on their team and you can think it over. . . . Now ya ask what's wrong with Drysdale and he's pitched too much and I didn't make a success with my pitching staff because they had a bad year all along with myself and . . ."

It that clear?

STOLEN BASE. *See* Steal.

STREAK. A batter is on a streak when he has hit safely in a number of games in a row. A team is on a winning (or losing) streak when it has won (or lost) a number of games in a row. A hitter is said to be a streak hitter or streaky if he does most of his hitting in clusters.

The most famous hitting streak was by Joe DiMaggio, who batted safely in 56 games in a row in 1941, a record many observers feel will never be equaled. Pete Rose hit safely in 44 games in a row as a Cincinnati Red in 1978 to set the modern record in the National League.

The longest winning streak by any team was by the New York Giants, who won 26 straight games in 1916. The longest losing streak was 23 defeats in a row by the Philadelphia Phillies in 1961.

STRIKE. A pitch that passes through a prescribed zone. Whether a pitch is a ball or a strike is determined by the umpire. A strike can be achieved in the following ways:

1. A pitch is swung at by the batter and missed.
2. A pitch enters the strike zone and is not swung at.
3. A pitch is fouled by the batter when he has less than two strikes.
4. A pitch is bunted foul.
5. A pitch touches the batter as he swings at it.
6. A pitch touches the batter when he is leaning into the strike zone. It doesn't matter if he has or hasn't swung at the ball.

Note: A strike of another sort has been introduced to baseball—by the umpires (when they went on strike to improve their lot in 1979) and by the players (when they struck in 1981 over the issue of free-agent compensation). *See* Major League Baseball Players Association.

● *The umpires call strikes on batters; they also call strikes on major-league baseball, as they did in 1979 when they struck for a better contract.*

STRIKEOUT. When a batter is sent back to the dugout, charged with three strikes. Sometimes called whiffing or fanning a batter. The ultimate in effectiveness for a pitcher. Nolan Ryan holds the record for having struck out the most batters in one season (383) and shares with Tom Seaver and Steve Carlton the record for having struck out the most batters in one 9-inning game (19).

STRIKE ZONE. That space over home plate that is between the batter's armpits and the top of his knees when he assumes his natural stance. A pitch must be thrown in that zone to be called a strike if it isn't swung at by the batter.

SUBMARINE. An underhand delivery. A difficult pitch, since the pitcher throws from a raised mound. Submarine pitchers are a vanishing breed. The most recent ones to use this delivery with any effectiveness have been Ted Abernathy of the Cubs, Braves, and Reds; and Dan Quisenberry of the Royals. Ballplayers, in describing Abernathy's motion, used to say, "He comes from out of the ground."

SUN FIELD. That part of the outfield where the sun shines most, making the position more difficult to play. The most notorious sun field in baseball is left field at Yankee Stadium during October—World Series time. Many teams have been beaten there by fly balls lost in the sun.

SUPERSTITION. Baseball has bred many superstitions, including the belief that finding a hairpin brings a base hit, spotting a wagonload of barrels or hay gives good luck, a pitcher who strikes out the first batter will be sure to lose, the man who leads off an inning with a triple will stay on third base without scoring, and the player who makes a sensational fielding play will be the first to come to bat the following inning.

Most superstitions are out of date, but some live on—ballplayers and managers still wear the same shirt or tie throughout a winning streak, avoid number 13 or else make a point of wearing it, and insist on touching or not touching a certain base when they go on and off the field.

Leo Durocher, when he coached at third base, always made certain to erase with his spikes the chalk markings that bordered the coaching box. An almost universal superstition among players is their avoidance of any reference to a no-hit game if a pitcher is in the process of pitching one, although many pitchers who are not superstitious will take pressure off by mentioning their own no-hitter.

Somebody once asked Babe Ruth if he had any superstitions. "Just one," the Babe said. "Whenever I hit a home run, I make certain I touch all four bases."

SUSPENDED GAME. A called game that at a later date is to be continued from the point when it was suspended.

SWINGING BUNT. A ball hit by the batter that dribbles slowly. It's not meant to be a bunt, but, after a full swing, the ball travels no farther than a bunt.

SWITCH-HITTER. A batter who swings from either side of the plate, hitting left-handed against right-handed pitchers

● *Mickey Mantle demonstrates the art of switch-hitting.*

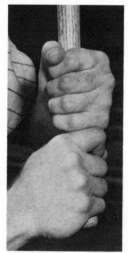
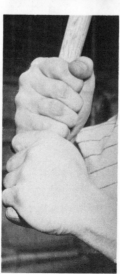

and right-handed against left-handed pitchers. At one time switch-hitters were rare, and for years the only truly successful ones were Frank Frisch and Red Schoendienst. Then along came Mickey Mantle to switch-hit with such amazing success that switch-hitting became the vogue. Pete Rose became the first switcher to achieve 3,000 base hits. During the 1965 World Series the Los Angeles Dodgers presented an infield in which all four members—Wes Parker, Jim Lefebvre, Maury Wills, and Jim Gilliam—were switch-hitters.

TAG. The action of a fielder in touching a runner with the ball, with his hand, or with his glove holding the ball to register an out.

TAG UP. When a fly ball is hit, a runner on base can "tag up," meaning he can try to advance to the next base after the ball is caught. He must, however, have his foot on the base until the fly is caught before attempting to advance.

TAKE. To let a pitched ball go by without swinging. When a coach wants a batter to let a pitch go, he gives the take sign. Youngsters often use "taking a pitch" to mean swinging at it, but in professional baseball the meaning is just the opposite.

TATER. Ballplayers' slang for a home run, arrived at by a long process. Originally, "tater," slang for potato, meant a baseball,

just as "pill," "apple," and "seed" did. Later, a home run was a "long tater." Then it was shortened to "tater."

TEXAS LEAGUER. A looping fly ball that drops safely just beyond the infield and just in front of an outfielder. So called because before the turn of the century the parks in the Texas League were particularly small. Puny hits of this and other kinds are also known as sea gulls, dying swans, bloopers, bleeders, banjo hits, and scratch hits.

TEXAS RANGERS. Billy Martin came to Texas as Ranger manager in 1974 and made a series of bold predictions. "We will win, we will contend, and we will draw a million fans," brash Billy said. People laughed; after all, the Rangers had won only 111 games in their two previous seasons.

But Billy Martin proved a prophet. The Rangers, led by league MVP Jeff Burroughs, Rookie of the Year Mike Hargrove, and pitchers Fergie Jenkins and Steve Foucault, were in contention all summer and finished with 86 victories, just four less than world champion Oakland. And the team drew over 1,000,000 fans.

It was a glorious time for a franchise that had begun as the Washington Senators in 1961. When the American League expanded to 10 teams, the old Washington Senators moved to Minnesota and the new team was started in the nation's capital.

But the stay there was relatively short. After 11 years of sagging attendance and

141•

● *Ranger second baseman Bump Wills is in the tradition of his famous father, Maury, who was a Dodger star.*

mounting losses, the team moved to Arlington, Texas, in 1972. After two disastrous years the 1974 turnaround appeared to be the start of something big. But Martin's magic soon wore off and the Rangers lost more games than they won in 1975 and 1976.

Their finest year came in 1977 when youngsters Jim Sundberg and Bump Wills led the team to 94 victories, a club record. The Rangers finished second in the American League West.

The team became a puzzle as the 1970s drew to a close. Every year the Rangers were picked to finish near the top of the division, and every year the Rangers were a disappointment. Not even the hitting of Al Oliver, who batted .319 or better in three straight seasons from 1978 to 1980, could make the team a contender.

THIRD BASE. The base to which the runner heads after having reached second base safely. It is located diagonally to the left of home plate and is 90 feet away from home and 90 feet away from second base. The player who covers third base is the third baseman.

THUMBED OUT. To be banished from a game by an umpire for any number of reasons, most common of which is disputing a call. A ballplayer thrown out of a game is said to have been thumbed, given the thumb, chased, ejected. Joe Garagiola tells a story about his arguing with an umpire and growing so angry that he threw his catcher's mask 20 feet into the air. "If that mask comes down," said the umpire, "you're out of this game."

TOE PLATE. A piece of leather (previously metal) sewn to the pivot shoe of a pitcher to protect the shoe. It is necessary because the pitcher drags his pivot foot after making his pitch.

TOOLS OF IGNORANCE. The catcher's equipment: mask, chest protector, and shin guards. They are so called because a catcher is so prone to injury that it is said that only the ignorant would choose such a position.

TOP. The first half of an inning, as in the top of the ninth. Also used in newspaper headlines to mean one team defeating another. For example, "Dodgers Top Cardinals, 4–3."

success on the field, winning only 54 games, baseball had arrived as a major sport in Toronto.

There were some bright spots that first season. Infielder Bob Bailor, the Jays' first pick in the expansion draft, batted .310, and third baseman Roy Howell hit .302.

The next year the Blue Jays upped their victory total from 54 to 59 after acquiring slugger John Mayberry from the Kansas City Royals. Mayberry and Otto Velez combined to give the Blue Jays a potent lefty-righty punch.

The Blue Jays had their finest year in 1980 when new manager Bobby Mattick guided them to 67 wins. Pitchers Jim Clancy and Dave Stieb combined for 25 victories, and the double-play combination of Damaso Garcia and Alfredo Griffin was among the league's best.

● *The Blue Jays' John Mayberry socked 30 homers in 1980.*

TORONTO BLUE JAYS. The experts snickered when the American League announced it had awarded a franchise to Toronto in 1977. The weather was too cold, the park was too small, and there was no guarantee that people in the Canadian city would take to major-league ball.

But at the end of that first year it was the Toronto management and the American League that had the last laugh. The Blue Jays drew over 1.7 million fans to cozy Exhibition Stadium (capacity 43,737). Though the team was somewhat less than a

TOTAL BASES. The total number of bases credited to a batter on his base hits—a single giving him one base; a double, two bases; a triple, three bases; and a home run, four bases. Babe Ruth's 457 total bases (85 singles, 44 doubles, 16 triples, and 59 home runs) made in 1921 are a record for one season. In 1954 Joe Adcock of the Milwaukee Braves made 18 total bases in one game on four home runs and a double.

TRADING DEADLINE. That time of year after which teams are no longer allowed to trade players, although players may be sold through waivers after that date. June 15 has been the trading deadline in recent years. (*See also* Waiver.)

TRIPLE. A three-base hit. Also a three-bagger. The triple is the rarest of base hits, combining power and speed on the part of the hitter. It is not surprising, therefore, that the record for three-base hits for a career is 312, less than half the record for home runs. The records for three-base hits in each league, coincidentally, were set in the same year—1912. J. Owen Wilson smacked 36 triples for the Pittsburgh Pirates that year to establish the National League record, and Joe Jackson of the Cleveland Indians set the American League record (tied two years later by Sam Crawford of the Detroit Tigers) with 26. Crawford holds the career record of 312.

TRIPLE CROWN. If a player leads his league in batting average, runs batted in, and home runs, he wins the Triple Crown. There is no trophy for it, but it is one of baseball's rarest honors. Only nine men have won it—two of them twice. The nine: Jimmie Foxx, Athletics, 1933; Lou Gehrig, Yankees, 1934; Rogers Hornsby, Cardinals, 1922, 1925; Chuck Klein, Phillies, 1933;

Mickey Mantle, Yankees, 1956; Joe Medwick, Cardinals, 1937; Frank Robinson, Orioles, 1966; Ted Williams, Red Sox, 1942, 1947; and Carl Yastrzemski, Red Sox, 1967.

TRIPLE PLAY. The act of retiring three men in one sequence, rare in any form but especially if it is an unassisted triple play, only eight of which have been made in the majors. In 1927 two were made on successive days by Jimmy Cooney of the Chicago Cubs and Johnny Neun of the Detroit Tigers.

TRIPLE STEAL. All three base runners stealing a base on the same play.

TV AND RADIO. Baseball broadcasters have added their own pet expressions to the game. Red Barber contributed "sittin' in the catbird seat" to describe a team or player in position of advantage, and "squeaker" for a close game. Exclamations like Mel Allen's "How about that?" and Phil

● *Mel Allen was a popular New York Yankee broadcaster.*

● *Tony Kubek (left) and Joe Garagiola, both ex-players, are longtime announcers for NBC-TV's Game-of-the-Week.*

Rizzuto's "Holy cow!" are frequently mimicked when something odd or sensational happens.

Barber and Allen were the first of the well-known baseball broadcasters. In later years ex-ballplayers moved into the field with extraordinary results. When Frankie Frisch called the New York Giant games, he used to repeat his favorite expression, "Oh, those bases on balls!" Dizzy Dean rambled delightfully along about outfielders who "throwed" the ball and runners who "slud" into third.

Following the lead of Frisch and Dean and Waite Hoyt in Cincinnati, ex-players took the airwaves by storm. Phil Rizzuto, Jerry Coleman, Ralph Kiner, Tony Kubek, Joe Garagiola, Bill White, Don Drysdale, Bob Uecker, Buddy Blattner, Richie Ashburn, and Johnny Pesky became regulars behind the microphone.

Baseball went on the air in 1921, when Graham McNamee broadcast the World Series between the Giants and the Yankees over the radio. The Chicago Cubs instituted regular-season broadcasts in 1924, with Hal Totten at the microphone.

Television entered the field in 1939, with

Barber doing the commentary on a game between the Dodgers and the Reds in Brooklyn. Today television is big business for ballclubs, and every team in the major leagues and some in the minors broadcast and telecast at least some of their games.

TWEENER. A ball hit between two outfielders (up the alley), usually a double or triple, sometimes an inside-the-park home run.

TWI-NIGHT. A one-admission doubleheader consisting of a twilight game (starting at about 6:00 P.M.) and a night game immediately following the twilight game.

UMPIRE. One of the officials who administer the rules. Umpires have been called arbiters, men in blue, Blind Toms, and worse. Usually there are four umpires for a game, one at home plate (he is the umpire in charge of the game, calling balls and strikes as well as any play at home) and one each at first base, second base, and third base. For a World Series two umpires are added, one down each foul line. Umpires are chosen by the league president to work in the World Series, and it is considered a reward, because there is extra money to be made from the assignment, not to mention the prestige.

The umpire is a much abused individual, yet any player will admit the game would be a joke without strong and courageous umpires. That was the way it was until the 1920s, when along came a stern individual named Bill Klem to give the umpire new stature and respect. Klem is most famous for his comment: "I never made a wrong call in my life."

Like a player, an umpire starts out in the minor leagues and is scouted by the major leagues. The good ones make it to the big leagues.

An umpire's life is a lonely one. While a player spends half his season in his home ballpark, the umpire is almost always on the road during the season. He must stay at hotels other than the ones the players stay at, and he must never be seen associating

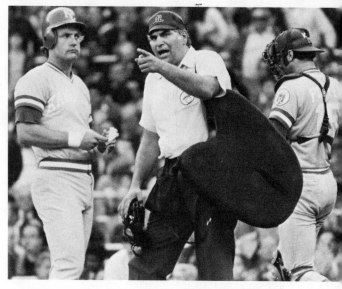

● *George Brett listens as umpire Ron Luciano renders an opinion. Luciano has since left balls and strikes for a career as a baseball announcer.*

● *Emmett Ashford was the first black umpire in the majors.*

with players. An umpire earns between $18,000 and $50,000 per year plus traveling expenses. He must purchase his own uniforms and equipment, at a cost of about $1,000 every three years.

UNIFORM. The players' whites, grays, flannels, or monkey suits. The New York Knickerbockers wore the first uniforms in 1849. For years the uniforms were standard, white ones for the home team and gray ones for the visiting team, and all uniforms were made of flannel. With the start of night baseball, the Cincinnati Reds and the Brooklyn Dodgers experimented with a satin uniform for night games. Now uniforms come in pastel shades of various textures, and some teams even use a sleeveless uniform shirt, such as the Oakland A's, who vary their three-piece uniforms in three colors: kelly green, Fort Knox gold, and wedding gown white.

UP. The team at bat or the player at bat. Traditionally, the game begins when the home-plate umpire cries, "Batter up!"

● *The Oakland A's are having their victory party in 1974 after winning their third straight World Series. Announcer Joe Garagiola is on the left, Reggie Jackson in the center, with manager Alvin Dark on the right.*

VICTORY PARTY. It is traditional that the team that wins the pennant or the World Series celebrates with a victory party in the clubhouse after the winning game. The highlight of the party is the uncorking of champagne, most of which is poured on the players' heads instead of in their mouths. Often the players continue the victory party long after they leave the clubhouse, sometimes with disastrous results.

After one pennant-clinching the Yankees continued their celebration on the train returning to New York. Pitcher Ryne Duren got into a playful mood and smashed a cigar in the face of Ralph Houk, then a Yankee coach. Houk became manager some years later, and early in his first season Duren was traded.

The Pittsburgh Pirates clinched the 1960 pennant and kept their party going on the bus back to the hotel from the ballpark. Another playful guy innocently tugged at the foot of Vern Law, the Pirates' ace pitcher, and accidentally sprained Law's ankle. The ankle was still sore when Law pitched in the World Series. Favoring the ankle, he put added strain on his pitching arm and developed a sore arm that almost ended his career.

WAGNER, HONUS. To baseball card collectors, shortstop Honus Wagner is the biggest name of all. A model of clean living in his playing days of 1897–1917, Wagner demanded a tobacco company's baseball card of himself be withdrawn from the market because he didn't want to be associated with smoking. The card, which had only limited distribution and therefore is a collector's item, is now worth from $10,000 to $15,000, depending on its condition.

Wagner, who was born in Mansfield, Pennsylvania, on February 24, 1874, was the finest shortstop of his time. He compiled a lifetime average of .328 and won eight National League batting titles, all with the Pittsburgh Pirates. In 1936 he was among the first group of players selected for the Hall of Fame. He died in 1955.

WAIT OUT. When a batter waits for a type of pitch he prefers to hit. In waiting out a pitcher, the hitter will often try to foul off strikes until he receives his favorite pitch or forces the pitcher to walk him.

WAIVER. The means by which a team can sell a player or send him to the minor leagues after the cutdown date. The team places the player's name on a waiver list and he becomes available to the other clubs. If none of the other teams—which select in the reverse order of their standing—claim him, the player may then be sent to the minors. If a player is claimed, his team must either remove his name from the list and keep him or sell him to the claiming team for the waiver price of $20,000. After the trading deadline, a player cannot be sent from one team to another without first being cleared through waivers.

WALLY PIPP. To say this to a player is a reminder that if he sits out a game, he may never get his job back. It comes from Wally Pipp, a Yankee of the 1920s. Pipp, the regular first baseman, got sick on June 1, 1925. His place was taken by a young man named Lou Gehrig, who did not miss a game thereafter until May 2, 1939. Gehrig played in a record 2,130 games in a row, and, of course, Wally Pipp never got his job back.

WASTE ONE. When the count on the batter is strongly in the pitcher's favor, the pitcher might waste one (throw one deliberately out of the strike zone) with the hope of getting the batter to swing at a bad ball.

WHIZ KIDS. The name given to the Philadelphia Phillies of 1950, who surprised everybody by winning the National League pennant. Not one of the starting players had yet reached his thirtieth birthday, thus the name Whiz Kids, a variation of "Quiz Kids," a popular radio show of the time that featured a panel of child prodigies.

WILD PITCH. A legally delivered ball thrown so high and so wide of the plate that it cannot be handled by the catcher and results in a base runner moving up one or more bases. It is charged against the pitcher as simply a wild pitch, not an error. There can be no wild pitch if there is no runner on base or if a runner does not advance.

It is interesting to note that the most wild pitches made in an inning was four, by Walter Johnson, one of baseball's greatest pitchers, which gives rise to the thought that a little wildness is a good weapon because it may cause batters to be afraid to dig in at the plate.

WILD THROW. A fielder's erratic throw that enables a runner or runners to advance one or more bases. Unlike the wild pitch, a wild throw is scored as an error even if it is by the pitcher.

WILLIAMS, TED. It was the final home game of an otherwise unmemorable 1960 season for the Boston Red Sox. Yet it had special meaning because, at age 42, Ted Williams, perhaps the greatest pure hitter in baseball history, was retiring. This would be his last appearance at Fenway Park, where he often feuded with critical fans.

On this day Williams gave the critics something to remember him by. In his final at-bat he sent a huge home run over Fenway's right-field fence, a final exclamation point to a truly remarkable career.

Williams was born on August 30, 1918, in San Diego, California, and came to Boston to stay in 1939, breaking in by winning the league runs-batted-in crown with 145 and hitting .327. A year later he raised his average to .344. In 1941 he wrote baseball history, soaring to a .406 average. Forty years later no other player had come within 16 points of that accomplishment.

Going into the final day of the 1941 season, Williams' average stood at .3996 and manager Joe Cronin offered to keep him on the bench to protect the .400 he had before a doubleheader against the Philadelphia A's. Williams would have none of that. He played in both games and tacked the final six points onto his average with six hits in eight at-bats.

• *Ted Williams hit .406 for the Red Sox in 1941, and nobody has hit .400 since then.*

That was the first of six batting titles for Williams. Twice—in 1942 and 1947—he won the Triple Crown, leading the league in batting, home runs, and runs batted in. He was passed over for the MVP Award in both of those seasons and also in 1941, his .406 season, when Joe DiMaggio won it for hitting in a record 56 straight games. Williams did win MVP crowns in 1946 and 1949.

When he won the 1958 batting title with a .328 average, he was 40 years old, the oldest man to be a batting champion. He finished with a career average of .344 and that farewell Fenway Park homer gave him 521, third highest in history at the time.

WINDUP. One of the two legal pitching positions, the other being the stretch position. A pitcher winds up when there are no runners on base, or runners are on third, or second and third, or the bases are loaded. He stretches at all other times. The stretch is a short windup and insures against a potential base stealer taking too big a lead.

WINNING PITCHER. The pitcher credited by the official scorer, according to the rules, as the winner of the game. It is what all pitchers strive for. In the case of a starting pitcher, he must pitch at least five complete innings to receive credit for a victory. A relief pitcher may pitch to only one batter and still be the winning pitcher if, while he is in the game, his team goes ahead and stays ahead.

WORLD SERIES. The fall classic and the climax of seven months of work beginning with spring training, in which the champions of the two major leagues meet in a best-of-seven series, the winner called the world champion. It has been held every year since 1903, except for 1904, when John McGraw, manager of the lordly New York Giants, refused to let his team play the upstart Boston Red Sox of the new American League.

The World Series operates on an alternating schedule, opening in the American League city one year and in the National the next. After two games the Series shifts to the other team's park for the third, fourth, and, if necessary, fifth game. If more than five games are needed to determine a winner, the Series goes back to the first park.

Among the most memorable Series incidents were: Babe Ruth's pointing finger, which may or may not have predicted the home run that followed against the Chicago Cubs, in 1932; Brooklyn's Mickey Owens' failure to hold a third strike in 1941, opening the gates for a New York Yankee ninth-inning uprising and ultimate victory over the Dodgers; Cookie Lavagetto's game-winning two-out double in the ninth inning for the Dodgers, spoiling Bill Bevens' no-hitter for the Yankees in 1947; and two unbelievable catches—by Al Gionfriddo of the Brooklyn Dodgers against Joe DiMaggio of the New York Yankees in 1947 and by Willie Mays of the New York Giants against Vic Wertz of the Cleveland Indians in 1954.

Two of baseball's rarest rarities popped up in the World Series—an unassisted triple play by Bill Wambsganss of Cleveland in 1920 and Don Larsen's perfect game for the Yankees against the Dodgers in 1956.

Champions

Year	A. L. Champion	N. L. Champion	World Series Winner
1903	Boston Red Sox	Pittsburgh Pirates	Boston, 5–3
1904	no World Series		
1905	Philadelphia Athletics	New York Giants	New York, 4–1
1906	Chicago White Sox	Chicago Cubs	Chicago (AL), 4–2
1907	Detroit Tigers	Chicago Cubs	Chicago, 4–0–1
1908	Detroit Tigers	Chicago Cubs	Chicago, 4–1
1909	Detroit Tigers	Pittsburgh Pirates	Pittsburgh, 4–3
1910	Philadelphia Athletics	Chicago Cubs	Philadelphia, 4–1
1911	Philadelphia Athletics	New York Giants	Philadelphia, 4–2
1912	Boston Red Sox	New York Giants	Boston, 4–3–1
1913	Philadelphia Athletics	New York Giants	Philadelphia, 4–1
1914	Philadelphia Athletics	Boston Braves	Boston, 4–0
1915	Boston Red Sox	Philadelphia Phillies	Boston, 4–1
1916	Boston Red Sox	Brooklyn Dodgers	Boston, 4–1
1917	Chicago White Sox	New York Giants	Chicago, 4–2
1918	Boston Red Sox	Chicago Cubs	Boston, 4–2
1919	Chicago White Sox	Cincinnati Reds	Cincinnati, 5–2
1920	Cleveland Indians	Brooklyn Dodgers	Cleveland, 5–2
1921	New York Yankees	New York Giants	New York (NL), 5–3

1922	New York Yankees	New York Giants	New York (NL), 4-0-1
1923	New York Yankees	New York Giants	New York (AL), 4-2
1924	Washington Senators	New York Giants	Washington, 4-2
1925	Washington Senators	Pittsburgh Pirates	Pittsburgh, 4-3
1926	New York Yankees	St. Louis Cardinals	St. Louis, 4-3
1927	New York Yankees	Pittsburgh Pirates	New York, 4-0
1928	New York Yankees	St. Louis Cardinals	New York, 4-0
1929	Philadelphia Athletics	Chicago Cubs	Philadelphia, 4-2
1930	Philadelphia Athletics	St. Louis Cardinals	Philadelphia, 4-2
1931	Philadelphia Athletics	St. Louis Cardinals	St. Louis, 4-3
1932	New York Yankees	Chicago Cubs	New York, 4-0
1933	Washington Senators	New York Giants	New York, 4-1
1934	Detroit Tigers	St. Louis Cardinals	St. Louis, 4-3
1935	Detroit Tigers	Chicago Cubs	Detroit, 4-2
1936	New York Yankees	New York Giants	New York (AL), 4-2
1937	New York Yankees	New York Giants	New York (AL), 4-1
1938	New York Yankees	Chicago Cubs	New York, 4-0
1939	New York Yankees	Cincinnati Reds	New York, 4-0
1940	Detroit Tigers	Cincinnati Reds	Cincinnati, 4-3
1941	New York Yankees	Brooklyn Dodgers	New York, 4-1
1942	New York Yankees	St. Louis Cardinals	St. Louis, 4-1
1943	New York Yankees	St. Louis Cardinals	New York, 4-1
1944	St. Louis Browns	St. Louis Cardinals	St. Louis (NL), 4-2
1945	Detroit Tigers	Chicago Cubs	Detroit, 4-3
1946	Boston Red Sox	St. Louis Cardinals	St. Louis, 4-3
1947	New York Yankees	Brooklyn Dodgers	New York, 4-3
1948	Cleveland Indians	Boston Braves	Cleveland, 4-2
1949	New York Yankees	Brooklyn Dodgers	New York 4-1
1950	New York Yankees	Philadelphia Phillies	New York, 4-0
1951	New York Yankees	New York Giants	New York (AL), 4-2
1952	New York Yankees	Brooklyn Dodgers	New York, 4-3
1953	New York Yankees	Brooklyn Dodgers	New York, 4-2
1954	Cleveland Indians	New York Giants	New York 4-0
1955	New York Yankees	Brooklyn Dodgers	Brooklyn, 4-3
1956	New York Yankees	Brooklyn Dodgers	New York, 4-3
1957	New York Yankees	Milwaukee Braves	Milwaukee, 4-3
1958	New York Yankees	Milwaukee Braves	New York, 4-3
1959	Chicago White Sox	Los Angeles Dodgers	Los Angeles, 4-2
1960	New York Yankees	Pittsburgh Pirates	Pittsburgh, 4-3
1961	New York Yankees	Cincinnati Reds	New York, 4-1
1962	New York Yankees	San Francisco Giants	New York, 4-3
1963	New York Yankees	Los Angeles Dodgers	Los Angeles, 4-0
1964	New York Yankees	St. Louis Cardinals	St. Louis, 4-3
1965	Minnesota Twins	Los Angeles Dodgers	Los Angeles, 4-3
1966	Baltimore Orioles	Los Angeles Dodgers	Baltimore, 4-0
1967	Boston Red Sox	St. Louis Cardinals	St. Louis, 4-3
1968	Detroit Tigers	St. Louis Cardinals	Detroit, 4-3
1969	Baltimore Orioles	New York Mets	New York, 4-1
1970	Baltimore Orioles	Cincinnati Reds	Baltimore, 4-1
1971	Baltimore Orioles	Pittsburgh Pirates	Pittsburgh, 4-3
1972	Oakland A's	Cincinnati Reds	Oakland, 4-3
1973	Oakland A's	New York Mets	Oakland, 4-3
1974	Oakland A's	Los Angeles Dodgers	Oakland, 4-1
1975	Boston Red Sox	Cincinnati Reds	Cincinnati, 4-3
1976	New York Yankees	Cincinnati Reds	Cincinnati, 4-0
1977	New York Yankees	Los Angeles Dodgers	New York, 4-2
1978	New York Yankees	Los Angeles Dodgers	New York, 4-2
1979	Baltimore Orioles	Pittsburgh Pirates	Pittsburgh, 4-3
1980	Kansas City Royals	Philadelphia Phillies	Philadelphia, 4-2
1981	New York Yankees	Los Angeles Dodgers	Los Angeles, 4-2

• *It's a merry moment for the world champion Pittsburgh Pirates after they ousted the Baltimore Orioles in 1979.*

X. Used in box scores, this means something out of the ordinary. For instance, if a runner has reached first base on a call of catcher's interference, the box score will read X—Rose. At the bottom of the summary a line says: X—reached first on catcher's interference. In baseball standings an X before a team in the listing means that the club has won its division title.

YASTRZEMSKI, CARL. The ball wended its way past Yankee Willie Randolph's vacuum-cleaner glove at second base. Carl Yastrzemski limped down the first-base line, favoring an aching Achilles tendon. But for those 90 feet between home plate and first base, the pain took a back seat in this game in 1979. And when the man they call Yaz pulled in safely at first, he had achieved his three-thousandth hit, a milestone in itself but all the more significant because he became the first player in the American League ever to combine 3,000 hits and 400 home runs.

Red Sox fans exploded with a roar of approval for the left fielder who had followed in the footsteps of the legendary Ted Williams at Fenway Park.

Yastrzemski was born on August 22, 1939, in Southampton, New York, the son of a Long Island potato farmer who was determined that Yaz would get an education. After his freshman year at Notre Dame, Yaz signed a $100,000 bonus contract with the Red Sox in 1958. But he pledged to complete the courses necessary for his degree.

• The one and only Yaz—Carl Yastrzemski— captured Boston's Fenway Park faithful in a career that began in 1961 and was still going strong in 1981.

And eventually he got his diploma at Merrimack College near Boston.

Yastrzemski came to the Red Sox in 1961 following Williams' retirement. But it wasn't until 1967 that Yaz won the fans over with a remarkable year in which he became baseball's last Triple Crown winner. He batted .326, with 44 home runs and 121 runs batted in, leading the league in all three departments. In the final two games of the season, when the Red Sox won their Impossible Dream pennant, Yaz had seven hits in nine at-bats as Boston beat Minnesota to clinch the flag.

His batting championship that season was the second of the three Yaz has earned in his career. He has batted over .300 six times and is among the leaders in many batting categories.

YOUNG, CY. In 1890 a young pitcher warming up against a wooden outfield fence in Canton, Ohio, did enough damage to cause someone to remark that it looked "like a cyclone hit it."

A sportswriter picked up the phrase and so Denton True Young was dubbed "Cy." He was born in Gilmore, Ohio, on March 29, 1867, and nobody has come close to matching some of the records Young compiled in his 22 seasons in Cleveland, St. Louis, and Boston.

His 511 victories are 95 more than Walter Johnson's second-best total. He also holds the mark for complete games (756) and innings pitched (7,356). Young, who pitched three no-hitters, was elected to the Hall of Fame in 1937. In 1955, shortly after he died, baseball named its top-pitcher award in his honor.

The award is given by the Baseball Writers Association of America to the best all-around pitcher in each league. Until 1967 there was only one award—to the top pitcher in the majors.

153 •

Cy Young Award Winners

(Before 1967 only one pitcher won an overall major league award.)

Year	Player, Club	Year	Player, Club
1956	Don Newcombe, Brooklyn Dodgers	1962	Don Drysdale, Los Angeles Dodgers
1957	Warren Spahn, Milwaukee Braves	1963	Sandy Koufax, Los Angeles Dodgers
1958	Bob Turley, New York Yankees	1964	Dean Chance, Los Angeles Angels
1959	Early Wynn, Chicago White Sox	1965	Sandy Koufax, Los Angeles Dodgers
1960	Vernon Law, Pittsburgh Pirates	1966	Sandy Koufax, Los Angeles Dodgers
1961	Whitey Ford, New York Yankees		

NATIONAL LEAGUE

Year	Player, Club	Year	Player, Club
1967	Mike McCormick, San Francisco Giants	1975	Tom Seaver, New York Mets
1968	Bob Gibson, St. Louis Cardinals	1976	Randy Jones, San Diego Padres
1969	Tom Seaver, New York Mets	1977	Steve Carlton, Philadelphia Phillies
1970	Bob Gibson, St. Louis Cardinals	1978	Gaylord Perry, San Diego Padres
1971	Ferguson Jenkins, Chicago Cubs	1979	Bruce Sutter, Chicago Cubs
1972	Steve Carlton, Philadelphia Phillies	1980	Steve Carlton, Philadelphia Phillies
1973	Tom Seaver, New York Mets	1981	Fernando Valenzuela, Los Angeles Dodgers
1974	Mike Marshall, Los Angeles Dodgers		

AMERICAN LEAGUE

Year	Player, Club	Year	Player, Club
1967	Jim Lonborg, Boston Red Sox	1974	Jim Hunter, Oakland A's
1968	Dennis McLain, Detroit Tigers	1975	Jim Palmer, Baltimore Orioles
1969	Mike Cuellar, Baltimore Orioles	1976	Jim Palmer, Baltimore Orioles
	Dennis McLain, Detroit Tigers	1977	Sparky Lyle, New York Yankees
1970	Jim Perry, Minnesota Twins	1978	Ron Guidry, New York Yankees
1971	Vida Blue, Oakland A's	1979	Mike Flanagan, Baltimore Orioles
1972	Gaylord Perry, Cleveland Indians	1980	Steve Stone, Baltimore Orioles
1973	Jim Palmer, Balitmore Orioles	1981	Rollie Fingers, Milwaukee Brewers

• **Cy Young pitched the most victories in baseball history—511.**

ZIP. Another word for a shutout, used mainly in newspaper headlines. Newspapermen writing headlines like the word because it is the shortest way to say "shutout."

• **Facing page: The Dodgers' Fernando Valenzuela won the Cy Young Award in 1981.**

Index

Page numbers for photographs are in *italics*.

Photograph Credits

All the photographs in this book are from United Press International with the exception of the following: Clifton Boutelle, pages 90, 103 (top); Ken Regan/Camera 5, pages 42, 98; Thomas DeFeo, pages 36, 46 (bottom); Malcolm W. Emmons, pages 18, 30, 64 (top), 78, 80, 81 (bottom), 146 (bottom); Mitchell Reibel/Fotosport, pages 2, 34, 91, 117, 129, 143, 155; George Gojkovich, pages 39, 49, 81 (top), 137; Nancy Hogue, page 89; Ronald C. Modra, pages 54, 118; Richard Pilling, pages 1, 14, 35 (bottom), 38, 41, 46 (center), 65, 77, 106, 124, 131, 132, 142, 146 (top); Baseball Hall of Fame/Sports Photo Source, page 97; Bob Feller Collection/Sports Photo Source, page 58; CBS-TV/Sports Photo Source, page 93; NBC-TV/Sports Photo Source, pages 62, 145; Sports Photo Source, pages 25, 66, 88 (top), 92 (top), 113 (bottom), 127; Wide World Photos, pages 55, 83.